IRREALITIES, SONNETS & LACONICS

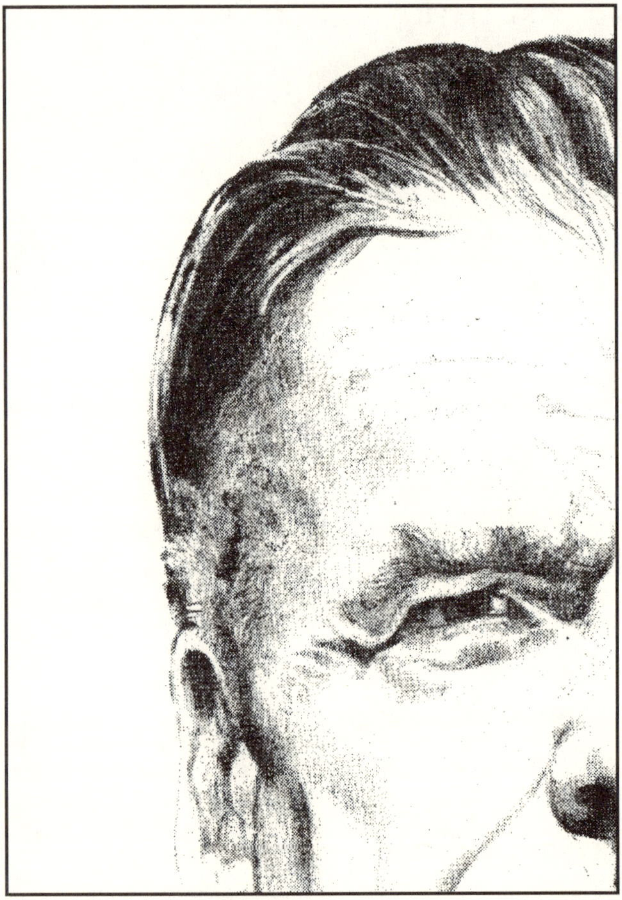

Irrealities, Sonnets & Laconics

Edited with an Introduction by

BARRY CALLAGHAN

with the assistance of Gregory Betts

TORONTO

Exile Editions

2003

This edition is published by Exile Editions Limited,
20 Dale Avenue, Toronto, Ontario, Canada M4W 1K4

Sales Distribution:
McArthur & Company
c/o Harper Collins
1995 Markham Road
Toronto, ON
M1B 5M8
toll free:
1 800 387 0117
(fax) 1 800 668 5788

Composition & Design by *Michael P. Callaghan*
Typeset at *Moons of Jupiter, Toronto ON*
Cover Painting by *Bertram Brooker*
Cover Design by *Tim Hanna*
Cover Drawing by *Dennis Burton*
Interior Drawing by *David Annesley*
Printed and Bound at *Gauvin Imprimerie, Hull QC*

ONTARIO ARTS COUNCIL
CONSEIL DES ARTS DE L'ONTARIO

The Canada Council for the Arts since 1957 | Le Conseil des Arts du Canada depuis 1957

The publisher wishes to acknowledge
the assistance toward publication of
the Canada Council and the Ontario Arts Council.

ISBN 1-55096-561-1

The Word

The word resumes its power
in old integrity
and I can feel and see.
What is it that I feel?
What is it that I see?
A new integrity!

Introduction (unpublished) to *Laconics*

Not too abstruse. Recording, possibly a state of mind. Transmission of a state. Not always. Beyond realism? An attempt. Attempting. The way to lead, to be. Is there no answer? I asked, was there an answer. Ante and post. Meaning, meaninglessness. No meaning. In spite of declarations etc., etc.

What meaning? Beside the point;—but not impressionistic either. The irrational is.

October 1932

Contents

Annesley

After The Battle, The Dawn: A Critical Memoir

When I was a child my father took me across town to a red-brick corner house on Delaware Avenue. I have always remembered the street name because my father was telling me tales at night about the Delaware Indians.

He took me there for a girl's birthday party . . . a girl I didn't know. And there was a tall woman who had three names . . . Mary Lowrey Ross . . . a woman whose stride was loose and easy, whose voice was deep, whose laughter crackled lustily out of her throat, too much smoking *Players Mild.* She led me into the living room, a clutter of easy chairs, sofas, papers, books, cigarette ash. There were girls everywhere and I insisted I wanted to speak to the father of the house. A girl, Nancy, marched me to the hall. She pointed up the stairs. "He's up there, in the attic. He's up there all the time in the attic." The only attic I had ever seen was at the house of my three spinster aunts: empty picture frames and old death cards and wire dressmaker's mannequins and broken oil lamps, steamer trunks with rusted hinges, the dust floating in shafts of light from a small oval window.

I didn't know why a man would want to work in an airless attic room, so I remember agreeing to hold hands with the girls and we paraded around the dining room table wearing paper pirate's hats. Then, suddenly, there was a man standing over us, square-jawed, dressed in grey, his cheeks furrowed and grey. The sight of his skin felt like ash. He spoke to the tall woman and she smiled a little, and then without speaking to us he went back upstairs.

Years later, on every second or third Saturday evening, Eustace Ross arrived at our house. He fascinated me. I almost never heard his footsteps. He would come up the veranda stairs, his fedora plunked on his head, and grin at no one in particular, and then drift sideways into the room, making no noise. He always sat near the fireplace, in an antique chair, thin-boned legs and ribbing, the arms too high for comfort, but he liked to sit in it, stolid, incongruous, his elbows jutting out over the arms. He stretched his legs straight before him, the thick soles of his polished black brogues facing his friends.

He would sit for a long time in silence, and depending on his mood, his depressions, he would take no part in the early, quick bantering talk of the evening, or, he would defiantly break in, blurting out something sharp, even hurtful, as if he had been angered, slapped by a hand no one had seen (one night, Marshall McLuhan was explaining how important it was to understand that what was missing between images in dreams was the conjunctions — and Eustace, exasperated, suddenly hissed, "Listen for God's sake, he's explaining Freud to us, he's explaining Freud . . ."). Often, he mumbled a terse, clipped aside, a snipe rather than a sneer. He went in for ambush. I tried to sit near him. His quiet words were witty and cutting. They nearly always died unnoticed, and Eustace, his mouth squared by the lines of his jaw, would laugh, a wide and silent laugh. No one heard his joke, no one heard his laugh. Sometimes, this made him laugh even more, silently, so that he did not look like a dour, taciturn man who worked all day scanning meteorologic maps, incoming Highs, Lows. He looked mischievous, a little lunatic, a prankster lurking behind his grey clothes.

I remember my mother telling me that she had met Eustace at a party, following him down one of those long narrow halls in what used to be called railroad apartments, living room at the front end, kitchen in the middle, and sunroom at the back end. The hostess was bending over to get more quart bottles of beer from a box. She was a prig: Eustace, with a chuckle, had given the hostess a slap on the buttocks. "Up the Empire, up yours," he'd cried. My mother, who was not a prig, liked him immediately. She always talked to him. I learned over the years that most women found something attractive in Eustace; the feeling perhaps, that he had secrets to tell only them. Or perhaps — rare among men — he knew how to listen to women. Perhaps that's something he shared with my father: because my father knew how to listen to secrets. Women talked to him all the time. I certainly believed that there were profound secrets between Eustace and Mary. She was open and garrulous and full of confident laughter. She never seemed surprised by any gesture he made.

But there were men who resented Eustace. Bitterly. He was impossible if you were a businessman. He baited them. He brought out their bile. He would nearly always say something insulting. They complained that he was rude, that he needed a good punch on the nose. I somehow believed that his sharp, defiant insults were little revelations of a dangerous, desperate game — perhaps because he always winked at me — revelations of the intense capped feelings of a very lonely man, or rather, a man who felt least lonely when he was as alone as he could be, a man alone in the attic of his head.

I remember as a boy standing on the beach at Lake Scugog where he and Mary had their summer cottage, watching him lay out oars after a long row in their boat and I asked my mother where he had been and my mother said:

"He rowed across the lake and back."

"By himself?"

"Yes."

I stood for a long time staring at the dim outline of the opposite shore, like a grey water stain at the bottom of the sky, miles away, and I wondered why a man would row over there — all that distance — by himself and then row back and what thoughts would he have while rowing that hard all alone? What dark and prankish plans? What sharpening of the eye.

He was a prankster. When great public debates were going on in the city newspapers he would adopt the role of the colonial reactionary he abhorred. He wrote preposterous letters to the newspapers, curmudgeonly letters, bigoted, always supporting the British or Ulster Orange cause, ripe with diatribe and the usual ignorance. He signed them "Old Flag," knowing the Old Flag editors at the newspapers would eagerly print such nonsense. No one, except his Saturday night friends, knew who "Old Flag" was. No one really knew who Eustace was. No one knew that he had fought in the First World War, that he had been gassed in the trenches, that he'd suffered shell-shock. No one knew that he was a mesmerist who believed that during the Second World War he had received messages from spirits, messages that he took so seriously he wrote to the U.S. War Department warning them that there was going to be an invasion of western Ireland. The War Department had written back and told him to leave them alone but he had studied the note with his philatelist's glass and decided that several type-keys had been filed down, and after analyzing the flawed letters, he discerned another secret message, this one telling him to disregard the order, it was a deliberate deception, and to carry on! He did, writing poetry and receiving messages, not only from the dead but from Prime Minister MacKenzie King. "What a world," my father said — some years later — after we knew more about the spiritualism of the Prime Minister — "King was talking to his dead dog and at the same time he had Eustace on the line."

The only reputation Eustace had was among a few poets, relatively unknown themselves. He was the first modern poet in Canada — he was years ahead as a radical irrealist (his word) of the *automatistes* in Quebec, he was an experimental imagist (who makes the later Tish movement seem derivative if not redundant), and a formalist who gave new vigour to the old sonnet conventions — yet he was incapable of hustling editors and critics during the twenties and thirties. His work was never published by a commercial house, and in the fifties many editors forgot about him. He began to talk of his work as something he had put behind him, a waste of effort. He was ill at this time, deeply depressed, suffering trench sweats in his sleep, enduring shock treatments — electrodes attached to that attic mind — and after he recovered from this *whopping* of his brain, he refused to discuss his poetry.

Then one Saturday, the conversation shifted from the dopiness of Prime Minister Diefenbaker wanting to 'green' the tundra and the polar cap to the west coast poets, and Eustace sat in his usual chair — but on this evening his legs were drawn under, tucked, and he was hunched forward; and he took apart — almost line by line — Ferlinghetti's *A Coney Island Of The Mind* — "all that kind of so-called surrealism, it's really just a kind of sloganeering, images as slogans, insanity and the end of the world as whimsy. That's its charm, that's why it's so wonderfully light-headed, it's so available. Surreal slogans." Eustace knew what he knew. He read and translated from the French (Max Jacob became a kind of other self), German (Heine and Holderlin, whose peculiar lyrical bent — his "impersonal voice of the heart" — he could not quite capture), Italian (Dante, who did not suit his gifts at all), Latin, and Spanish. He had a first-rate eye and a critical mind. The next day I searched my father's library for a little volume I had long ago thumbed through, a privately printed book of Eustace's verse. I found *Laconics*, and *Sonnets* and two ochre issues of *Poetry (Chicago),* one featuring "Irrealistic Verses" by W.W.E. Ross, 1934, and the other — "Modern Thoughts In Disguise" by Marianne Moore, 1933:

> In magazines favorable to innovation, Mr. W.W.E. Ross is conspicuously one of the writers of this

day. It is therefore not surprising that these sixty-nine sonnets (privately printed) should have freshness, responsibility, and authenticity of locality. They are about the oak, the pine, the lake, the river, the Indian, injustice, the supernatural, death, art, the Muses. In being proffered, some of them as imitative of Dante and of Italians before him, their modesty is appropriate but only conduces to an augmented conspicuousness. It is plainly 'one of the writers of this day' who gives us sonnets *1* and *2, To the English Language,* and no one could have made the following sonnet without having boldly faced the difficulties that to verse belong:

Prometheus, bound in adamantine chains
To the grim rock stark-lifting from the sea,
Watching with eyes that wandered ceaselessly
The sea and sky, the sky and sea; whose pains
Not yet become a torment in his veins
Were still sufficient, while in tension he
Awaited the strong hand of deity,
Expectant of some increase to his pains; —
Bound as he was, his eyes were growing dim;
Discouraged, he relaxed the effort vain
Of rude rebellion on that fatal day, —
When, like the dolphins in their lively train,
Gliding toward the rock in bright array,
The sea-nymphs sang encouragement to him.

There is present the Spenser-Sidney-Milton-Wordsworth elegance, and an ingenuity with dactyls, which recalls the Melic poets. To so staggering a roster of consanguinities with an occasional defect, one may demur, but poetry with the un-forced note is rare.

The next Saturday I told him I thought his poems were fine. He didn't want to talk, but persisting, I finally said, "Goddamn it, Eustace, they're good! What have you been doing up in that attic lately?" He invited me over to Delaware Avenue for drinks.

I felt silly on the evening. After all, Mary and Eustace had once stood over me as I stumbled around their dining room table, unhappily holding the hands of their little adopted daughters. They had watched me grow.

Eustace gave me drinks, nervous, prowling from chair to chair, awkward in his eagerness. Mary presided, a little bewildered that a young man should be so interested in forgotten images. We drank. We quipped. At last, I asked for the poems, and Eustace, hesitating only for a moment, disappeared up the stairs, and that was the only time I heard noise when he walked — those black brogues clumping up the stairs.

He showed me four ledgers filled with poems neatly written in ink, workbooks, the quality uneven, but many of the poems excellent. He seemed to have kept everything, hoarded each thought. I read aloud the poems I liked, and some I found astonishing:

After the battle the soldiers danced and ate up the
enemy's dead. No one tried to stop them. Help!
cried one of the corpses before it was devoured. The
way lay clear before them. Action dictated solely by

considerations of self-interest and one's own stomach consisted in doing just one thing. So that corpse too was eaten and the dance continued.

We drank a lot of scotch and he prowled back and forth, saying little, but he was pleased.

Some weeks later, I spoke about him on the radio, and read some of his poems . . . *the music that was heard Beyond antiquity. And sweeter than the call of bird in Spring's Iniquity.* But there was little or no response. Certainly none from the editors in town. Eustace had listened, and he told me, "You read them the way I would have read them." I was silly, he said, to expect any response.

Eustace was sick. My father muttered about "those damned shock treatments." But curiously, he seemed more at ease, more jovial, more like an amiable elf than a big clawing cat. He had been to death and back a couple of times. He was coming out of himself. Other poets were looking him up — a young fellow had come all the way from the prairies — and Eustace was full of strut, small strut, but strut. His face was no longer grey but white, which made the red stand out on his cheeks, and he seemed alive and over his depression. But the white was the color of cancer, and suddenly, Eustace Ross died.

It is a curious fact that imagism, as a movement, got kick-started in Canada. T.E. Hulme, the English literary theorist and poet, boarded a cargo boat for Montreal in July of 1906. Hulme crossed the Ontario north and the prairies. Struck by the vast forests and flat spaces, and knowing that the language of rumination and reverie had gone to seed on the sceptered isle he decided that what was needed to capture a landscape so raw was a language pared down and precise.

Hulme returned to England. Within a few years the imagists had broken the back of *Airy, fairy Lillian* and her limpid retinue on the Oxford road. It was a time — among those who cared — for Pound, H.D., Moore, cummings, Williams, and Amy Lowell. When Eustace began publishing in *The Dial* (1928) and *Poetry (Chicago)* (1934), he had turned not just to Pound but to Holderlin, René Char, Heine, and especially the surrealist Max Jacob — he had turned to images at the point where dream begins, images so spare, so direct, that they could make the dream concrete:

> *The old maid!*
> *She wears a black silk cape; she arrives with her*
> *lameness which supports her words and her hollow*
> *laugh.*
> *She comes into the garden, descending its scarcely*
> *marked slope.*
> *They thought she was lying down, very ill.*
> *"Well, since the doctor doesn't come to me, I'm*
> *coming to you, and I wish to say that I died this morn-*
> *ing at…but I can't find the words any more…*
> *Excuse me…if you see a flame in a bowl, it isn't*
> *melted candlewax, it's my soul…yes, indeed!?*
> *laughing, always amiable.*
> *"Good health to you all! I'm going away."*

Each word, each phrase was exact. There was no deliberate verbal complexity, no comfortable cosmic moralizing. The effect of unforced plain speaking was the essence, what Wordsworth meant when he said "there neither is, nor can be any *essential* difference between the language of prose and metrical composition . . . the most interesting parts of the best poems will be found to be strictly the language of prose when prose is well written." The concentrated eye is the key. Soldiers marching. A beggar. Angels. A flower. Trees, the lake, or a fish spine and rocks, exist in themselves, as "the fact the silence — only the silent fact," not as parts of any ideational design (he was at one with Williams, who said, "No ideas but in things"):

The white gum showing
in the gloom
along the massive
trunk of a great
pine-tree standing
on the hill
with a deep bed
of needles below.

There is a music in his lines, a music based on his ear for stress. It is a stringent music, sometimes not what it seems to be (he had an interest in syncopation, in the Blues monotony of the off-beat), sometimes complex. Try reading "Spring Song" on the down side of the first column — it starts with a stern two stresses per line, a regular marching beat on the 1-4, but try reading the song across, inserting the word *Momma* in the white space until you force yourself to read the space as a silence itself, and you are on the 1-3, the syncopated blues beat:

Spring Song

One day	*in the spring*
walking	*walking*
along	*the railroad track*
the track	*near the town*
I passed	*looking at*
a pond	*a pond*
slimy	*of greenish water*
greenish	*a large pond*
From it came	*incessantly*
sounds	*sounds*
of frogs	*frogs piping*
piping	*frogs in the water*
I picked up	*I could not see*
a stone	*any frogs*
and threw it	*I threw a stone*
into the pond	*into the pond*
The stone	*it splashed*
splashed	*a big splash*
and the piping	*and the sounds*
of the frogs	*the frog's piping*
stopped.	

This may seem slight to the casual reader, but it is not. Those silences are how he gave an unforced vitality to the everyday and how he entered into the surreal, too — they are the spaces McLuhan was talking about on that Saturday night, spaces where the conjunctions are left out — silent spaces enclosed / embraced by images that never become vague, images that are always hard. It's true that he had no ideas but in things, but I had never suspected how "courtly" a lover he could be in verse (who knows in life?), nor how committed he was to the dream made real by the word, nor had I quite understood while he was alive how acts repeated over and over as ideas — the deep plunge into the cold green element — could open up before his eyes so intensely for him — literally open up as flowers — and how blooms were not only an affirmation of life renewing itself in a cold land but an intimation of a May-leafing on the side of life that we call death. These intimations erupted out of the earth:

the densed grouped dandelion,
flames breaking patch-wise through
from inner suns beneath the soil…

These flowers, these flames, the explosive resurgence of life "alarms" — then strikes "terror" into the minds of those who have "denied this explosion" because the explosion is the spirit made "manifest in the world" —manifest to those who have tried to see a truth, to see

the wind
that blows from outer space
and from beyond,

a wind that

blows in through the hole
that the diggers have made in the wall.

Eustace died, went out through the hole in the wall when he was seventy-two. Among his last poems, there is a suggestion that the laconic long-distance Scugog rower — after a life of shock treatments — from little deaths to two Great Wars — and after a sojourn of being at play with Ezra Pound in the fields of Canto land — might be back:

> *Come ride in a boat past the shelving shore where the castle stands ruined and the ruins of the castle show sharp and black in the moonlight. Let us glide beyond the ruins, beyond the headland on which the castle once stood, around the headland past the sleeping village with the roofs of the houses shining a little in the moonlight; and going on as the boat glides down with the stream, on its dark surface, we may come at length to the land that we left once; and we may come to that land about dawn.*

Barry Callaghan

If Ice

If
ice shall melt
if
thinly the fresh
cold clear water
running shall make
grooves in the sides
of the ice;
if life return
after death
or depart not at death,
then shall buds
burst into May-
leafing, the blooms of May
appear like stars
on the brown dry
forest-bed.

1927

Issue

(translated from the French of Max Jacob)

The young girl—it is my soul—has been brought into my room by the four winged demons, her arms bound. They are going to saw her wrists. She faints. But Our Lord says: "Come this way for there are among the saints many children who resemble you." This way, it is snow! snow! snow! for Paradise is snow.

1932

In the Ravine

In the ravine   I stood
and watched the snowflakes
falling   into the stream
                         into the stream
flowing gracefully between
banks of snow
                         The black water
of the winter creek   came
around a bend   above
and disappeared
around a bend   below

Filled with melted snow
to the brim
the creek   came
around a bend—
and disappeared below
around a bend—
ground covered with snow

Thus I stood   the snow
descended   by degrees
into the stream
                    into the stream

1927

Kolto

(Translations from the Japanese by Lafcadio Hearn)

FIREFLY SERIES (HAIKU)

The lost child,
crying, crying,
nevertheless
catches fireflies.

✦

Out of the blackness
black people
call to each other—
they hunt fireflies.

✦

The fireflies,
pursued,
hide themselves
in the moonlight.

✦

Is it the glimmering
of festal fires
or is it fireflies?
Ah! the Genji! *(the largest type of firefly)*

✦

Is it the river
or does the darkness
drift with the stars?
Ah! the fireflies! *(by a great Japanese poet)*

✦

Not yet dark
and already
under the bridge
fireflies sparkle.

✦

A single firefly
having come
we can see
the dew in the garden.

✦

O fireflies gather
long enough
to show his face
who speaks to me.

(supposed to be
spoken by a woman)

✦

When evening falls
although my soul
burns more
than the firefly burns,
nevertheless,
as the light
of that burning is viewless
he is unmoved.

(supposed to be
spoken by a woman)

1925

Burial Conversation

(translated from the French of Max Jacob)

As a result of I don't know what circumstances, the celebrated Mr. X is attending this burial incognito. No one else knows him or recognizes him at the cemetery. Mr. X acknowledges my greeting; he comes over and speaks of my friend George:

"He deserves to be here!"

"Why, you hardly ever saw him!"

"Oh! you know George, when he has a good fire, a good bottle and a bad book. . . ."

"You're being too modest if you are speaking of yours."

"George doesn't read my books."

1932

The Cave

We live in a cave according to Plato and this seems to me true in another sense than that intended by him. In this cave is water and we reside on rafts or platforms peering down into it from time to time. When asleep we plunge into this water. Now, below the surface there is a passage leading from this cave into another cave, larger some say. Others maintain it leads into the open by the shore of a great sea. It is possible to swim through the passage but only on condition of not returning since it is too long apparently to be travelled both ways on the same breath. At least, no one has ever done so, except in fables and old stories.

On plunging down and swimming a little way into the passage a faint light—sometimes brighter—can be seen coming apparently from the farther end of the passage. No one however has found out much about this light—though some say they have seen other beings moving to meet them—because it is necessary for lack of breath to turn back speedily to our cave. Nor is it certain, some claim, what becomes of those who, swimming into the passage, do not return. Do they really go on to the other larger cave or reach the open sea-shore where all is light and beauty; or do they meet some other fate? Some think that the light is only a mirage and, so, deceptive.

Perhaps it is better thus, for if it were certain that at the end of only a short journey through the underwater passage we should reach the sunlit great sea, all would without hesitation plunge in and make the trip. As it is, it is forbidden to do so deliberately. What is the reason? All this is still a mystery.

1939

Curving, the Moon

Curving, the moon
over the mirror lake;
the new moon
thinly curving
over the lake.

Below, the pine
standing dark and tall,
through its black
topmost branches
the curved limb
of the new moon.

Rising, it leaps from the ground
immobile—
the dark pine
moon-illuminated
on the shore
of mirror-lake.

Is it a breeze?
No sound from the pine,
but on the water
a long shadow
ripples.

1923-29

from ***The Rooster and the Pearl***

(translated from the French of Max Jacob)

Picture of grandpa by a five-year-old: an ox-head smoking a pipe. The family is delighted: grandpa is annoyed.

. . .

Heavy fruit on a dwarf tree, much too heavy for the tree.

. . .

The archangel struck by lightning had only time to loosen his tie; one would have said he was still praying

. . .

date unknown

Metroge

A cube a sphere an octahedron.

The shining cube, the shining sphere, the octahedron glows with a dull light.

The shining of the cube reflecting the radiant energies dropped from the sun; the glittering of the smooth sphere; the discontentment of the octahedron.

"Sphere" he said "and cube, I know both of you and know you well as the moon knows its other side that we never see. But what of the octahedron?"

The answer was, briefly, this. "Granted the existence of a certain favouritism among the more geometrically abstruse figures; in spite of this the preferment shown not being welcome could not therefore be tolerated and the only alternative appeared to be the elimination of either one or the other."

A cube a sphere an octahedron.

1928

View

From a hilltop, in the spring,
I saw woods and valleys green
With new foliage, glistening
Streams winding in between

Meadows soft to walk upon,
Deep with fresh grass, golden too
With the dense-grouped dandelion,
Flames breaking patch-wise through

From inner suns beneath the soil.
In those woods, I knew, were hidden
Many wild birds, musical,
To the eye of man forbidden

But not to the ear, for often when
A silence holds the carrier air,
Listening, and yet again,
I have heard the music there.

1927

Exhortation

(translated from the French of Max Jacob)

The Breton—it is I—seated in the midst of the flags of the world. The moon carries a star in its hollow. The Breton pursues his studies among the flags of the world and an angel has come down towards him. "Stop your reading if God is still willing to visit you." God! You know my sufferings! What is that written beside your arm, angel with a woman's arms? Three Hebrew letters that I cannot read. When I have the Holy Spirit will he give me the gift of tongues?—

The angel is furious to see me so stupid.

1932

On Flowers

Who shall proclaim the mysteries of flowers
Exhaling odours "sweet as if in pain"—?
Yet with no sighings, nor do they complain
Under the sting of inner secret powers.
Perceiving them from garden-guarding towers
From which we gaze toward the open plain,—
Each flower on the earth can but remain
A little while to decorate some hours.
There in the garden see them in order stand.
Theirs is the full sweet share of sunlight strong
Even to the end of sunlight, and the night.
Theirs is the crowning of the smiling land
And all this picture will remain so long
As they shall drink the circumambient light.

1932

The Flower

Springing into
bloom the flower
alarms striking
terror into minds
having denied this
explosion.

1929

The Middle of Life

(translated from the German of Friedrich Hölderlin)

With yellow pears
And full of wild roses
The land hangs into the lake,
You lovely swans,
And drunk with kisses
You dip your heads
Into the holy and calm water.

Woe to me! Where can I
Find, in winter, the flowers
And where the sunshine
And shadows of earth?
The walls stand
Speechless and cold, in the wind
Weathercocks clatter.

date unknown

On the Hill

On the hill walking
I heard—
This was the woods and the shadows
and a flat expanse of muskeg as in the north
recalling
days while surveying
while moving with the surveying party
the soft deep moss the small
trees dotting the swamp
Then the woods the coolness the darker
way among the underbrush—
when I heard
being in uniform a soldier
proceding to the port of embarkation
to Europe and war
I heard
in the distance summoning
sweet, sweet clear the bugle.

1925

August at Sea

Deep engines
working smoothly,
drive the ship
toward France
across the water
of the channel.
It is night
and very calm.

The sea is calm;
and no stars
are reflected there—
the sky is clouded.
All the decks
are filled with soldiers,
reinforcements
for the front.

The sea is calm.
It is very dark
under the clouds
and we see
far over the water
a steady flame—
a vessel burning
in the night.

1925

Alexandria

Lost city, once an empire's capital,
When Alexander paused awhile from war
His leaping thought cast forth into the far
And dimly lighted future; as in thrall
Of visionary powers he saw all
The very earth, this dark and teeming star
Hail the proud conqueror in his battle car
As he went forth from the great city's wall;
But did he see that fate-engendered hour
When conquering Saracen his way should hold
Even into the lordly city's side?
And did he envisage the great caliph's power
Sweep like a tide, resistless, rude and bold
At length to humble even all that pride?

1932

from **The Rooster and the Pearl**

(translated from the French of Max Jacob)

At the foot of the bed, the mirrored wardrobe is a guillotine; there you can see our two sinful heads.

. . .

I saw my former professor of rhetoric, with a woman. I saw only their heads eating chocolate éclairs, with no pleasure: the big head of boredom and the little commandant's head. Oh! Oh! Revenge of humanity on the humanities. Well, I could hardly keep from laughing in revenge: Revenge of the humanities on humanity.

. . .

Mystery in this life, reality in the other; if you love me, if you love me, I'll make you see reality.

. . .

Paradise, I imagine, because of the number of dead, is like a mid-lent day in Paris, and hell like the distracted crowd of families in a port on the day of a storm.

date unknown

Headquarters

A chateau down in the village;
a latrine up on the hill
for thirty soldiers at once
if they wanted to use it at once.
Officers went in and out
of the chateau with red on their caps.
There was a bathroom too
a mile or so down the road
and thirty soldiers at once
were taken to bathe in the heat
of the water heated and ready
to rinse off the dust of the journey
up from the base in the little
French boxcars marked
FORTY MEN OR EIGHT HORSES.

1925

from **The Rooster and the Pearl**

(translated from the French of Max Jacob)

And when, of the Polish lancer, limbs cut off, bottle broken, there remained only an eye, the eye sang "The Two Grenadiers."

. . .

In a madman's hat, the knife-grinder (it is Death) opens a mantle lined with cherry-red silk to draw forth a big sword. A butterfly on the wheel stops him.

. . .

I dreamed that nuns set out garden plots in the church of the Sacred Heart, because God loves the earth, and sowed them with confetti because He loves joy.

. . .

date unknown

Butterfly

Butterfly
making for
flowers to
suck the sweet
juice of the
blossom

how great
then is your
pleasure in
all your
wandering

course among
colours and
greenery
through the sweet-
scented
aerial

path of your
fluttering
wings—
now in the
languorous
summer!

1923-29

After the Battle

After the battle the soldiers danced and ate up the enemy's dead. No one tried to stop them. "Help!" cried one of the corpses before it was devoured. The way lay clear before them. Action dictated solely by considerations of self-interest and one's own stomach consisted in doing just one thing. So that corpse too was eaten and the dance continued.

1937

Soldiering

Marching   the man
soldiers going along with drums
over the earth, over the earth

to kill   yet
is the air
sweet and clear
the sun rides and the wind glides

                    They
with keen blades go
marching   marching
over the earth

while the sun rides
and the wind glides.

1927

The Animals All

The animals all collected and agreed to a truce for one year. How happy they were! The lamb should no longer eat the lion. The tiger was safe before the ferocity of the squirrel. The chipmunk promised to spare the elephant. The beaver, who lives in water and cuts down trees most busily, took solemn oath that his sharp teeth should not be used on the crocodile. And so on; they were extremely courteous in agreeing to such arrangements. All beasts glowed with rectitude, and the occasion was one of the most marked harmony. Nevertheless, in spite of the favour with which this agreement was regarded, all seemed to find it better at the end of the year to revert back to the old arrangement, or lack of it. The squirrel, greatly to his relief, felt free again to attack the tiger, and the lion was no longer safe from the lamb.

1937

Nothing Has Changed

The four of them were playing rummy in Elmira's flat. They more or less made two couples. But all were against marriage.

The other girl was less handsome than Elmira who regarded herself as in complete command of the situation.

Danny Lee had always wanted to go to Hollywood and try his luck there writing scripts.

He went. That left three.

The two others got married or engaged. That is a terrible betrayal and shock to Elmira.

Elmira thinks she's losing her grip, slipping.

She heard from Danny Lee. He wasn't doing so well. He came back.

At first Elmira had the idea that all would go to Hollywood. She abandoned this idea after the betrayal.

Then she hoped Danny wouldn't do well there.

Elmira and he became secretly engaged, not telling the others. That gave her a feeling of security again.

"If they get married we'll spring our news too."

Elmira now felt she could have them all together again.

The four of them were playing rummy pinochle in Elmira's flat. Nothing was changed except that the partition into couples was a little more definite. The only difference now was that they formed more definitely two couples. Elmira was no longer in complete command of the situation but the next best thing to it.

date unknown

Sappho

When Sappho leaped to death for Phaon's sake
Off the Leucadian promontory down
Into a pitiless sea, did the skies frown
And Jove aver an anger then and shake
The lands he ruled? Did earth and sea awake
From their dull slumber? Did each Grecian town
Feel a deep sigh regretful, and trees blown
Moan to their depth and a deep tumult make?
Say! Did the earth groan at this profanation
Of song and music? Or did the land and sea
Assume their old untroubled rest again,
Unmoved, in their old tranquility,
And sea and land, every listening nation
Keep silent, heedless, with no tremor then?

1932

Good Angels

Good
angels
pause
they remain
still a
moment
If they shall
remain
a moment
If angels
If they should
more than
But no
they do not
more than
Good angels
touch
then pass

angels
pausing
a moment
do not fly
away
away now
perhaps
more than
more than
momentarily—
remain
a moment
no
do not remain
momentarily
pause
in a moment
are gone

1928

The Pipes of Pan

The pipes of Pan along a river's edge,
Clear and shrill and magic to the ear
I heard, and stood alone, alert, to hear
The sounds that seemed to come from clumps of sedge;
I heard again those notes along a ledge
Of lofty rock where one would feel great fear
On looking down, nor should approach too near,
With faltering step, the steep abysmal edge;—
Melodious, sweet, the sounds still echoed from
The neighbouring hills and ran through valleys wide.
The whole world stirred. Each creature in its home
Felt some strange lure that tempted it to fly,
And wander far, with towering hills beside,
Until the time when these live things should die.

1932

One Man

One man cannot fight many devils. There was a certain case. The recipient of stolen goods knew him by sight. When he approached the neighbourhood took on a strange carelessness as if nothing mattered much. His words were weighed down with much irony. Through the clefts which reason had bored into his mind came some sort of white light. Nevertheless the devils were close behind with persuadings to doubtful deeds and whirling thoughts.

1937

Identity?

Daemons and spirits of the world between—
What are you? Never has there been reply
Final to that old query sent constantly
To the dim region of strange things unseen,—
Whether the dead, as some assert, have been
Throughout the channels of the inner sky,
Made into beings of another dye,
Transformed to creatures of no earthly mien;—
Some say, you are the spirits of the dead.
The zone between, is it not thronged with those
Who once upon the earth pursued their way,
More active centres spiritual indeed—
Whatever some may doubtfully suppose
Them to be, or whatever some may say?

1932

Cotton Mather

I

"The devil lives
in Mexico," he said, "having
guided that land
the Indians

now dwelling there,
even as the Israelites
were led to the promised
land of old.—

Sacrilegious
imitation of
Jehovah acting
as leader to

his chosen people.
The Mexican devil
did even so,
and thus and thus."

II

Whenever he heard
the wind rushing in the forest
he muttered, "The devil
is abroad!"

He trembled at
thought of this strange land
and its strange
dwellers among

deep woods hiding
from white man's honesty.
He longed to burn
the forest and all within it

where, thinking, he saw,
driven by the wind,
witches flying
like dried leaves.

1939

The Tree

The tree whose sacred energy a spell
Exerts on him whoever beholds the tree—
And fixes his attention steadily
Assuredly some secret rich could tell,
For it must know, and hold the knowledge well,
Some process that involves undoubtedly
The very heart of Earth, and that must be
A vital centre able to compel.—
Tree-worshippers there are in Africa,
Men set apart to grow up with some tall
Tree of the forest, and they watch it grow,
Sinking into a trance, their minds away,
Drawn from the world; words from their lips will fall;—
They utter things that before they did not know.

1932

Prometheus—1

Prometheus who to men donated fire
And arts and crafts, given by him alone,
Against the will of Zeus's upstart throne,
Permitting even mortals to aspire,
Raising them from their state to something higher,—
Now bound by divine will against a stone
Before the vulture sent had fiercely flown
Against him to assail with talons dire;—
Even at that moment when his fate was fixed
And hope was none,—He knew it by his power
To see the future in prophetic sight,—
Even then he called out penalty unmixed
With pity upon that tyrant of an hour,—
How Zeus himself should be forced down to night.

1932

Prometheus—2

Prometheus, bound in adamantine chains
To the grim rock stark-lifting from the sea,
Watching with eyes that wandered ceaselessly
The sea and sky, the sky and sea; whose pains
Not yet become a torment in his veins
Were still sufficient, while in tension he
Awaited the strong hand of deity,
Expectant of some increase to his pains;—
Bound as he was, his eyes were growing dim;
Discouraged, he relaxed the effort vain
Of rude rebellion on that fatal day,—
When, like the dolphins in their lively train,
Gliding toward the rock in bright array,
The sea-nymphs sang encouragement to him.

1932

Efficacy of Confession

(translated from the French of Max Jacob)

On the road to the racetrack there was a beggar who looked like a servant. "Pity me," he would say, "I am vicious. I'll go and gamble away the money you are going to give me." And he would continue his confession.

He was very successful and he deserved it.

1932

Poem for a Song

(translated from the French of Minou Drouet)

for B.B.

I gathered three leaves of autumn
and made of them my boat
and the belly of the sea
remains stained with blood.

I gathered three rays of moon
for the rigging of my boat
and the garment of the sea
remains embroidered with pearls.

I gathered the trunk of an oak
to make the tall mast
and all the heart of the sea
resounded with its cry!

I gathered three birds of foam
and wove of them my sail
and against the sky's cheek
it's gliding like a tear.

The night has gathered three dreams
for the luring of my boat
the beating life of the sea
has drowned the whole with delight.

The nylon of sky and of waves
has closed upon my boat
nothing remains but, at sunrise,
a tear the colour of blood.

19x

The Watcher Speaks—2

"One night I saw a bright star fall from heaven
Beaming more powerful than many moons,
Like that most fervent sun on hot noons
Bends his strong glance until the hour of even.
Ah! It was fairer than the fabled seven,
The Pleiades, who, with celestial tunes,
Turn in their spheres as smooth as wind-swept dunes
Where keen and polishing winds have strongly striven.
'A spirit is come to earth' I loudly cried,
'Come to make merriment and careless glee,
To drive away the darkness from beside
The hearts of men that sleep and never wake,
To quiet all the winds upon the sea,
And sing the beauty of the mountain lake.'"

1932

The Tower

Into the blackness of the tower proceeded the band of sufferers who knew only where they were and whither going. The guides paused with whips caressing the stones, the grey heaviness; and all the time the beams, the ancient doors, the cells, the windows leading up and out into the hollowness of the inverted sky gave forth no sound but the footsteps of walking men. Mice running to and fro might prefer the coming of silence. "The well is deep," said the leader. "Water is a profound and secret thing. Time covers all and yet there is nothing hidden." So the remnant of the band led unwillingly down the steps emerged into the secrecy of the startling night and the singing stars.

1937

War

Often we
heard the
rumours of
war and the
sound of the slaughter.

This was in
Europe the
old, on the
fog-bound
coasts of the
continent.

Slaughter of
youth in the
fields,
sodden and
ground into
mud.

This was the
tragedy
O of the
young in
spirit.

1926

In the Forest of Silence

(translated from the French of Max Jacob)

In the forest of silence the night is not yet come and the storm of sadness has not yet injured the leaves. In the forest of silence, whence the Dryads have fled, the Dryads shall return no more.

In the forest of silence the brook has no more waves for the current runs nearly without water and changes course.

In the forest of silence there is a tree black as black and behind it a bush that has the form of a head and which is in flame, and which is in flame with the flames of blood and of gold.

In the forest of silence where the Dryads shall return no more there are three black horses; these are the three horses of the wise kings and the wise kings are no longer on their horses, nor elsewhere, and these horses speak like men.

1932

Stars

I saw
the stars   Aldebaran
Algol   and Alioth
        flaming

in distance
Suns

Names Arabian   those old
astronomers   saw

Algol Alcyone
in thc night
glittering afar
each point of light, each star.

1927

Lovers

We shall be
lovers of
all that is
lovely and
gentle and
bold

Fearing no
death but the
lapse of our
souls and the
sluggardly
peevish

Death that curves
mouldering
out of the
mouths of our
idleness

We shall be
lovers of
stars and the
light of the
full round moon

When in her
splendour she
rises at
set of the
sun.

1926

The Lover Plaineth the Absence of His Love—1

How oft thy dwelling have I passed today
As yesterday, whilst thou art far from home,
Musing upon this problem, how I may
Find thee therein, though well I know thou'rt gone.
Gazing upon the window that looks from
Thy chamber I still try to see thee where
The sunlight-riddled shadows go and come
Beneath the vine that waves its leaflets there.
Vain is the effort, vain the feeble plan;
No sign of thee within, I must confess,
Although my eye most eagerly doth scan,
Striving to make thee out of nothingness.
My eye gives up the task, my heart a stone,
My slow sad steps I backward turn, alone.

1932

V.

(translated from the Latin of Catullus)

Lesbia, let us live,
and let us make love, Lesbia;
As for the advice
of aged and severe men,
We'll rate that
at the value of a penny;
For suns may set
and suns may rise again, but
When, for us,
our little light is over,
Night will fall,
when we must sleep forever.
Give me kisses,
a thousand, and a hundred;
A thousand more,
and then another hundred;
And still another thousand,
and then another hundred;
Then let us kiss on,
not counting, for I'm fearful
The envious may know
how many thousands follow.

1926

CIX

(translated from the Latin of Catullus)

Pleasant, my
life, yet you set
forth to me
this
the love
between us

and how this
love will
surely
last without
ending.

Great gods!
Grant that
she be
able to
promise truly

and that she
says it
sincerely
and from the
heart.

that to us
all of our
lifetime
it may
continue
unbroken—

this
undying
pledge of
sacred
friendship.

1926

On Love

Love's the chameleon—always changing.
    What
We say of love holds good but for a time.
Love's an invention based in part on rhyme,
And love's own forms are various as is
    Thought.
There is no uniformity. We stop
At no one stage. No image is sublime,
But sentimental to the succeeding time—
All's different to the new who are newly taught.
Love changes; all's commotion, fashions all.
At one time we may talk of stars and such;—
Plato had views on love, most mystical,
But other views are possible to each.
Animals, too, no doubt, have their own views,
And Plato's views, to them, would be rare news.

1932

Dew

Dew! Dew! On every flower and every lead in the early morning of the woods, on every spider-web too, making each fine strand show white and the whole a delicate visible pattern. Dew! Dew! The distillation began at some undetermined time in the night. The moist air growing chilled exuded forth these essences. Dew on a lake would be superfluous. Dew on sand, dew on a sandy road through the woods. At any rate, the sun is not long up before his slanting rays search out the fragile fine drops, and colouring each prismatically they nevertheless disperse them all by degrees, the rainbow colours leading only to annihilation. And after rain, too, where is the dew?

1932

Pine Odour

A perfume sweeter
than odours brought
from eastern lands,
of rarest scent,
a perfume sweeter
than all of these
is the odour
of the pine;

Sweeter than scents
from eastern lands,
than odour of musk
from Turkestan,
than frankincense
from India,
than odour of myrrh
Arabian;

Or Mediterranean
myrtle berries—
the pine that stands
to breathe in the summer—
than odour of musk
from Turkestan,
than odour of myrrh
Arabian.

1932

Higher Degeneration

(translated from the French of Max Jacob)

The balloon is ascending. It is shining and is shaped to a point still more brilliant. Neither the oblique sun which directs its rays as an evil monster throws dice, nor the cries of the crowd—nothing will keep it from going up! No! The heavens and it are but a single soul; the heavens open only for it. But, balloon, take care! There are shadows in your car and they are moving, unhappy balloon! The aeronauts are drunk!

1932

Problem

A different reality, or view of reality. We can compare our view of a situation to a relief map. Certain things stand out. The supernormal view would produce a relief map at first sight unrecognizably different.

The Problem—to assimilate the two.

1937

Minoan

Here in a
garden we
see with a
delicate
foliage
pictured

Trees and their
leaves. O how
deft-drawn
light and
fantastic!

Faces of
men and of
women there
also,
figures of
women,

All in the
garden they
move among
delicate
foliage.

1926

The Neophytes

They walked in darkness through a passageway
Narrowly lying under the massive stone,
No sooner entered than the light was gone,
The amicable light of Egypt's day;
Once entered, thin and very far away
Did seem the light, as if forever flown,
And dreary darkness, dangerous, alone
Remained about the suppliant on his way.
The passage choked, but underfoot the floor
Sloped upward, gradually at the start—
Then steeply, turning, rising, until done
The difficult dark journey and the door
Opened upon the platform where did dart
The incomparable radiance of the sun.

1932

Mystery of the Sky

(translated from the French of Max Jacob)

On returning from the ball I seated myself at the window and gazed at the sky; it seemed to me that the clouds were immense heads of old men seated at a table and that they were brought a white bird with its feathers on... A broad river crossed the sky. One of the old men lowered his eyes towards me. He was going to speak to me when the enchantment broke up, leaving the pure sparkling stars.

1917-1923

The Stream of Life

Angelic figures gliding in the stream
Of life, with a celestial sky above,
Show forth, embody that great rule of love
There underneath the illuminating beam
That through this spiritual zone doth gleam,
Making, itself, those mobile natures move—
Though none against the benign current strove—
Through the bright regions where fair spirits teem;
Where all is calm. The motion quick employs
The energies ever of the creative light
That gleams and shows each heavenly nature young,—
The living light, mild, active, in the night
Even, of earth, most steadily fills with joys
Minds where a lasting melody is sung.

1930

The Call

A stranger ceremony than the antique call
On dead Osiris, living, to return
To those who called, whose very hearts did yearn
For clear response, not dim, but sure, to all
Their queries to the heavens dark and tall,
Regarded by these watchers keen to learn;—
The dead are gone, but yet the dead return.
There's no finality in a funeral.—
A stranger ceremony than that ancient one
Is now performed in darkened eager rooms
Where men and women sit; and one in trance;—
Waiting expectant till the answer come
Out of the gathering places of the gloom,
Not sinister, but comforting,—nor chill.

1932

from **The Companions in the Garden**

(translated from the French of René Char)

To André du Bouchet
and to Jacques Dupin

To a rose I bind myself.
The only master that may be favourable to us is the
Lightning, which now illuminates us and now rends us utterly.

Lightning and rose, in us, in their fleetingness, join for our fulfillment.

Their crime: an enraged desire to teach us to hate the gods
we have in us.

The real sometimes quenches thirst for hope. That is why,
against all expectation, hope survives.

To touch a dunghill with one's elbow...

When I dream and go on, when I hold the ineffable, waking,
I am on my knees.

What consoles me is that I'll be there when I am dead—
dismembered, hideous,—to see myself, poem.

1957

Death Nearing

"Death nearing
faint am I
dimly I
see and the
light is
diminishing

"Death and the
darkness—
increasingly
dark is the
day—

"Sinking I
swoon into
nothingness,
rapidly
now I am nearing

"Death and the
wings of the
spirits who
gathering
bear me up onward."

1927

On Angels

Angels, as well as birds, on silent wing
Proceeding through the upper, open air
Under the full intense celestial glare,
Perceive the true forms of each earthly thing;
Birdlike the eye they deftly, subtly fling
Into the distance. Steadily they stare
Unhindered by the circumambient glare,—
Angels as well as birds can sweetly sing.
They too are known to hover above a nest
Wherein the swathèd soul of man doth lie
Soft-hidden in the down of matter's wool,
And theirs, too, the prerogative of rest,—
To sooth at times in manner wonderful,
With kind and piercing glance of soul and eye.

1932

I Was Looking

I was looking at some words
culled from a dictionary
at random. All had meaning.
The question was, how to use them
when suddenly
the words blew up

sc (all) at (o) ter

(ve) e d S (r) cat (the)

ter (p) ed (a)

(g) (e)

and I realized
I had written a poem
by e.e. cummings

1955

Glimpse

Yours is that voice, that tone I hear
When in my inmost, rarest dream;
Yours is the face I see appear
In that mysterious gleam.

I hear you speak and often too
I answer feebly. In a land
Of strange dissolving unreal view
There in the light you stand

A moment only, then are gone
When I awake to ponder till
I sleep again what I alone
Have seen and heard and ponder still.

1927

Dream-Way

It may be that the country of a dream
Illuminated, or remaining dim or dark,
Resembles that low shore where souls embark
Into the zone where shades and shadows teem;
With no more than a momentary gleam
From higher spheres.—Before them, grim and stark,
They see a vessel on that water dark,
And all surroundings threatening, ominous seem,
It may be so, that Dream Death's brother is.
That dream, that region, all shall know some day
Or soon, the dream that merges into death.
The zone of dreams, now known, may be the way,
May be the path that surely leads beneath
To solving of these lasting mysteries.

1932

Warm Day

Warmth
of the day.   Hotness
of the sun.   Poised
in silence the song
of the bird awaiting
the coolness.

Insects whirr
wings glittering
and these are happy.

Sudden a breeze
a wave   of coolness
stirring leaves
            making
branches move.

Upon these wings to soar
rising out of the heat
and the bright dust
and the silent song.

1927

The Wise Men

From the Babylonian tower of old
Astronomers surveyed the passing sky—
Wise men they were—the noble company
Of silver stars, or else they were of gold;
And all the lore that they had often told
To one another, they told encouragingly,
And they found wonders in the heavens high
For quick to learn each new thing they were bold
And so they dwelt, weaving curious lore
Into the story of that ancient time
With nightly observation on the floor
Of heaven until a marvel appeared to them,
And awestruck at this newer wonder prime
The wise men saw the star of Bethlehem.

1932

Reciprocal

The shuttle swinging
to and fro;
the piston
of the locomotive
moving smoothly,
powerfully,
into the cylinder,
out of the cylinder;

dancers swaying
in one place;
crows' wings
in lazy flight;
waves on the ocean
up to the shore
and back swiftly
broken and foaming.

1925

The Pythagorean Basilica

They found an ancient church beneath the street,
Building mysterious, hidden underground;
Its dark recesses gave back hollow sound
To their pickaxes from below their feet.
Who were they that did here in secret meet,
In this deep refuge that the oppressèd found
A shelter from the dangers spread around,
Holding their treasured ritual complete?
For here were men and women intent upon
The mystery lying hid beyond the tomb.
Light from the past they sought and held it well.
And were they not as worthy of the sun
As those who in the open pronounced their doom,
Who held the bonds of power to compel?

1932

Ion

In the clear morning, in the temple court,
Stood Ion, guardian priest of the great god,
Not hesitating, vain or overawed,
Busy, although the time since dawn was short,
Calling upon the rest for full report
Of duties done, when done,—and, where he stood,
Washing the court, checking the impious brood
Of winged birds that stained the sacred spot.
So in the clearness of the morning he
Sang to the sun, Apollo, and the bright
Ruler of the day unceasingly until
Strangers he welcomed; thither, it might be,
From Athens or from Sparta, while, in his sight,
Blameless the god. His faith was perfect still.

1932

Rotation

One man saw two others seated by a fire.

The long journey that he made led him to an island clothed with pleasantness.

Leaving the island he was aware of a chilliness in the air and ice-bergs seemed to be approaching.

The strong-minded master of the ship yelled at the mate who had strong hands and between them they brought the ship to safety.

Landing, he passed through a wood where the dangers were so apparent it was superfluous for him to note the presence of fear.

Coming to the edge of the wood he saw two men seated by a fire.

1925

Golden Apollo

Never can disappear into a cloud
The golden god equipped with golden lyre.
Rapid his melody as celestial fire,—
His drawing near makes mortals call aloud;
At whose departure all the noble crowd
Of heroes, in their sacred new attire,
Would raise no voice melodious to the lyre
But droop their heads, silent in sorrow bowed.—
Apollo, leader of the muses nine,
The mistresses of poetry and song;—
Pure gold the instrument as empyreal light
Bright-beaming into radiance clear and fine
As are the rays of sunlight sweet and strong
While all the watchers marvel at the sight.

1932

Spring Song

One day
walking
along
the track
I passed
a pond
slimy
greenish
From it came
sounds
of frogs
piping
I picked up
a stone
and threw it
into the pond
The stone
splashed
and the piping
of the frogs
stopped

in the spring
walking
the railroad track
near the town
looking at
a pond
of greenish water
a large pond
incessantly
sounds
frogs piping
frogs in the water
I could not see
any frogs
I threw a stone
into the pond
it splashed
a big splash
and the sounds
the frogs' piping

1928

Let Us Rebuild

(translated from the French of Max Jacob)

It is enough that a child of five, in pale blue blouse, should draw pictures in an album for a door to open into the light, for the castle to be rebuilt, and the dry brown of the hillside to be covered with flowers.

1932

Sphere

A sphere. Hold it
in the eye.
The polished glass
surface attracts,
drawing the eye
into its centre
as it draws all
the light surrounding.

The sphere gathers
the light surrounding
into its polished
smooth surface.
Set the sphere
in the light of the sun—
it will give you
back the sun.

1928

The Vessel

The vessel was very liable to be wrecked. We knew that; but we took no measures to prevent it. No line was shot up by blazing rocket and no boats were launched to help the people in the vessel: in such deep distress. We knew they were. And yet they seemed singularly unconcerned. As the vessel drifted along the white line where a sharp rock cut the vibrating sea, they were seen dancing and we heard through the wind a sound of singing. "What people are those so inconsiderate, so heedless of their own destiny?" we cried in wonder, disapproving. But what we said or possibly thought made no difference whatever and we soon lost sight of the vessel as it moved on down the coast.

1925

Pacific

Turn to the
sunlit
Pacific and
not to the
fog-bound
Atlantic;

Face to the
new and the
light, not
back to the
old and the
heavy,

Heavy of
heart and of
mind with the
weight of an
aeon of
sad years.—

Turn to the
blue of the
sky and the
glitter of
sun on the
water,

Over the
ocean to
sail in the
search for a
joy
never-ending.

There in the
light in the
sun in the
open day
face to the
westward,

Striding
away from
all glooms
of the old
the relentless
continent.

This is a
race of the
west and we
hate the old
graveyards of
Europe.

1926

The Travellers

Two young travellers met at a cross-road and beginning a noonday meal of bread and wine began describing dream-castles to one another. A rivalry soon sprang up. Each tried to impress the other in his description of a dream-castle that he, personally, had seen and each tried to outdo the other in the elaborate beauty of his description. Soon there was quite a group of ignorant wandering passersby assembled around the two narrators who grew momentarily more and more heated and enthusiastic in their descriptions. Presently some of the group of auditors began asking precisely where these castles were situated, whereupon the two young men went into the matter in great detail saying at length what lands one passed through on the way, and giving each other the most minute directions for the trip. So worked up did they become under the stimulus of the interest and questioning that each finally, though at heart he knew his own story entirely illusionary, came to believe the other's story, whereupon they suddenly started up and set out in different directions, each towards the other's dream-castle, leaving behind them several loaves of perfectly good bread and several packages of cigarettes.

1928

On the Supernatural

We must affirm the supernatural
However doubtfully we have looked upon
Its bare existence in the time that's gone,
For it is ever near and ever real;
As we shall find. We love the natural.
The human reason seated on a throne,
Creator of kingdoms for itself alone,
Is conscious of no zone ethereal.
But to an end with all this lower view,
The cause illusory, vain and yet employed;—
Angels there are and kindly demons too,
Their throng, removed from faulty human sight,
In the unseen worlds as we should know in spite
Of natural explanation thin and void.

1932

The Cold Night

On cold nights the farmer builds higher the fire in the wood stove. Frost is forming on the window-panes; the wind sneaks in through crannies by the door and around the windows. All shiver if they leave for a time the stove's neighbourhood. The other rooms are chilly now. Only by the stove is there warmth.

Where are the dead on such a night? The farmer thinks of the graves, the graves so chill there beyond the woods beside the church. Where are the dead on such a night?

Is there a shadow at the window? Did the wind have an extra voice? Is someone speaking in the wind? The countryside is black. He goes to the door and looks. How black the countryside in the night! The wind comes rushing and goes on its way afar, afar.

1938

First Snow

Let the first
snow fall
white upon
fields and the
roofs of the
houses

freshly.
Let it remain a
time on them,
covering

all of the
dust, and the
dried-up
leaves of the
field-weeds,

hiding old
traces;
making all
new, for a time.

1958

Winter Scene

Black of the
branches and
white of the
snow that is
lying
upon them—

There I see
by the street
trees with
snow on their
branches;

New-fallen,
light, not
heavy with
liquid to
bending—

Black of the
branches but
white of the
new-fallen
snow.

1926

To Death

Chiefest of mummers and masked mysteries, Death,
Still stalking on the stage of humankind,
Uttering low threats against all who will find
In due time safety though they lose their breath—
Striding so fierce and vengeful; underneath
All hollow,—Who would fear, even if blind,
An empty shell, for we shall surely find
Death such unless much else is false and myth;
Away with all this mummery and worse!
We watch and shudder the dire ceremony
Fearing the sable plumage of the hearse
Barbaric, and the grave, that silent mound,—
For you, O Death, still frighten fearfully
Hinting we shall be held long underground.

1932

Skyscrapers, N.Y.

Lightness of
colour and
magic of
spires of the
lofty towers

crystalline
clear in the
light of the
dazzling
day

In the night
too they are
bathed in the
light of a
brilliant
flooding

singing their
songs in the
night, in the
silence of
night.

1926

To Tap the Wind

To tap the wind
that blows from outer space
and from the beyond—
the task confronting us now.
What is this wind that blows?
The spirit begins
to manifest in the world
and its ways are strange as ever
they were in times long past,
in ages long gone by.
Such are the ways of the sky,
and truth blows in through the hole
that the diggers have made in the wall.

1939

Flowers

Flowers
revolving in the sun
spinning colours
whirling
colours yellow
red and blue
and yellow

Flowers spinning in the sun
make the garden make one
garden in the sun.

These
upon stalks rotating
red brick-coloured
blood-coloured blue
yellow and pink

Flowers rotating in the sun
make the garden make one
garden in the sun.

1928

Little Poem

(translated from the French of Max Jacob)

I remember my childhood room. The muslin window curtains were worked with designs in white lace. I tried to find the alphabet there and when I made out the letters I would change them into figures I imagined. H, a man sitting down; B, the arch of a bridge over a river. There were in the room several chests with fully opened flowers carved in the wood. But what I liked best were the two rounded tops to pilasters that could be seen behind the curtains, which I looked on as the heads of dolls with whom it was forbidden to play.

1928

To the English Language—2

This English too can carry sweetest strain
Among the sweetest tongues and strongest too,
When we write carefully as seldom do
The writers of this day. Its old refrain
Once heard, will be remembered, heard again
In memory, its accents passing through
The zone of difficulty in the mind into
The inner cell of recollection plain.
And so among the tongues it must be placed
That most euphonious are, Italian, Greek,—
It too, this English that the nations speak
May be as musical as any tongue
Upon the singing earth; once boldly faced
The difficulties that to verse belong.

1932

Ovanuna Believed

(translated from the French of André Salmon)

Ovanuna believed that all
The birds in America were mechanical.

It is that lover's fault who, in order to teach you to spell,
Thought a trip every night to the movies would serve the
  purpose well.

Follow rather after me
To my beautiful castle dreamingly.
I will teach you, thanks to the differential calculus applied
  to space,
How skyscrapers really scrape
The sky so well and just in the right place;

That the sky
Bursting with laughter
Splitting with joy
Makes
Every forty years the earth tremble, and break—
So Frisco fell
A huge collapse whose echo over the wireless ran—
Like a steak shattering into seven pieces the frying pan.

1957

Laboratory

In the bright-lit
laboratory
the coloured liquids
glow in the light;
liquids in bottles,
or test-tubes or beakers,
of many colours,
or water-clear.—

The mystery
of measured matter,
with the aid
of crucible,
or test-tube held
above the flame—
the balance too,
above all else—

is sought by the workers
in this room—
the mystery
of measured matter;
the strict exactness
of the proportions;—
here coloured liquids
glow in the light.

1930

Moon

Over spaces
profound, un-
measured runs
the moon in flight
incomparable.
It is
now hidden by a
cloud. Now
visible. A sphere
so clear the full
heaven is not
more near.

1940

Wild Rose

Delicate
is the light
petal of
wild rose that
stands by the
pathway

Fragile and
delicate,
lightest of
pressure will
unbalance
fatally

Faintest of
touches will
start from its
base this light
petal of
wild rose

Delicate
fragile and
apt to be
swept away
suddenly.

1926

Night Scene

The lake is mirror-like tonight.
The trees on the bank
Dark, beautiful,
Look down at their reflections.

The water is shallow by the shore.
There reeds stand dimly seen,
Among whose roots
The wary pike lurks, waiting.

Perhaps a splash at the surface,
Perhaps a swift shadow
Will show where he pursues his victim
That cannot escape him.

Terror below the surface.
Beauty above,
As the exquisite dark trees
Gaze endlessly at their reflections.

1924

Visitant

If a spirit nightly come
From regions beyond air,
How shall it know its old home,
Descend a darkened stair?

How shall it know if lamps are lit?
How can it surely tell—
By sympathy remember it?—
The ancient humble spell

Of things familiar long before
In the once well-known house?
How shall it pass the fast-barred door
Or patiently arouse

The sleepers sleeping in their beds,
Laid out in level wise
With eyes close-fixed within their heads,
Unready for surprise

Of an unearthly visitant
Attempting to draw near
Who must continue hesitant,
As with a twinge of fear,

In old surroundings become strange
Through time and distance too,
And by the acid bite of change
Dimmed in the spirit's view?

Though spirit eye may range the sky
It cannot earthward move
Save on the bridge of sympathy
And long-enduring love.

1942

On Mythical Beauty

O all this beauty shall not remain obscured.
The older myths in which it is contained
Shall still reveal themselves; their form regained
Becoming ever clearer, not immured
Within the darkness that has long endured,
Nor shall the tension of a moment strained
Lose what the centuries have still retained,
What ages, though destructive, have assured.
Pure rays of sunlight from an earlier day
Will gently nurse forth shoots, tender at first,
Then stronger, from the illimitable soil,
Fecund, of the human spirit; in new ways
Will issue newer energies, to burst
Forth from their hiding place after much toil.

1932

Xerxes

Xerxes who
built a boat-
bridge on the
narrowest
part of the
Hellespont

hoping to
conquer the
Greeks, the
lovers of
freedom,

came to
disaster
near to an
island;
and let any
other

hopefully
artful
boat-bridge
builder
beware.

1940

The Whistle

A locomotive whistle in the night, sounding eerily. Lying awake and listening to that sound.

The sound was repeated. Through the darkness came the sound of the locomotive whistle; meaning a train moving somewhere out in the darkness of the world. Hearing the lonely sound, lying awake listening. But that was so long ago.

The sound came again perhaps or perhaps not again.

1932

Great Blue Heron

I

With snake-like neck
this swordsman stands
ready to drive
his long sharp beak
rapier-like
down into the water
to strike the fish
at which he is peering.

And I would fear
to meet this bird
in enmity
this rapid swordsman
so dexterous and
so powerful
with quick-straight thrust
from snake-like neck.

II

The great blue
heron standing
in shallow water among the reeds
watched the cat
creeping down the shore;
elongated
curved neck rigid,
the bird motionless
under the moon,
a dark erect
shape in the dimness
of reeds and water
in the moonlight;

until the cat
moved back up the shore
away, when the bird
resumed his slow
stiff forward stride,
neck extended,
peering down
and struck at a fish
with lightning beak.

III

The great blue
heron flappingly flying
out from the swamp where its nest
lies hidden always from prying eyes—

wild and shy,
anachronistic, almost, along
the summer lake's
shore, cottage-occupied—

moving slowly over
the lake, close by the shore, seeking
what? I do not know
why this bird sets out

leaving that spot,
the home, secret, unknown,
deep in the swamps,
dense-hidden in grasses and shrubbery,

but fearfully
watch the big bird, thinking
someone with a gun—
heard earlier, sharp in the morning—

may yet seek out
that refuge hidden through years
to end abruptly
its daily flying in freedom.

1939

102

The Snake Trying

The snake trying
to escape the pursuing stick,
with sudden curvings of thin
long body. How beautiful

and graceful are his shapes!
He glides through the water away
from the stroke. O let him go
over the water

into the reeds to hide
without hurt. Small and green
he is harmless even to children.
Along the sand

he lay until observed
and chased away, and now
he vanishes in the ripples
among the green slim reeds.

1939

Exhortation

(translated from the French of Max Jacob)

Be sad and fill the place where you live with outcries based on nothing but egoism. Be dutiful toward the demons of gloom and doubt. Sadness personified would wear a black cloak undoubtedly. In the archives of understanding there is a record of sadness too. Lamentations pierce the air shrilly with their repetitions like the little whistle attached to a peanut vendor's stand.

1937

On a Statue of Venus

Venus the mother, warm though carved in stone,
Looks calmly over the heads of those who fare
Through the great room; preserves for those who share
An admiration for the work of times long gone
A potent charm,—and love has ripest grown
In her. She gazes through the quiescent air,
Secluded somewhat from the noonday glare,
From her firm pedestal as from a throne.
Her look is calm, filled with serenity;
Her glance is kind as if towards a child;—
And yet this stone is cold, ancient and grey,
Lifeless would seem, encountered by the way;—
Of steady love maternal, fierce or mild,
She is the symbol in perpetuity.

1932

Andromeda

The large sun sinks. Across the wide calm sea
The red reflection creeps toward the rock
On which, pale as narcissus on its stalk,
Is bound the maiden gazing fearfully;
For Juno's and the Nereids' jealousy
And her fair mother's loud and boastful talk
Had brought her here to ward off the dread shock
Of Neptune's wrath. Her chains are plain to see.
Eyes wide in fright she stares at the setting sun;
She feels the night-breeze blow across her face,
And the rock hard and pitiless beneath.
Her heart is faint and of hope she knows none,
Awaiting in this drear and desolate place
The coming of the monster and of death.

1932

The Cloud

Over the body of the river hangs a cloud. It is colourless now if indeed it ever had a colour. Yet it moves although slowly along the river impinging occasionally on the trees that stand by the river. This fog would obscure a passage, preventing any crossing if it were not permeable to certain rays, to certain beams of a new light. And the lighting of the air, apparently from nowhere, grows in intensity until the cloud seems to be about to disappear. Down the river come rapidly two boats, propelled by oars. They come around a bend and glide past the point of observation. Their pilots and crews do not seem to observe at all the cloud lying so dangerously close above them.

1928

1931

I

Freight trains go slowly upgrade.
At the foot of the grade was a camp
Of biscuit-box metal, and slabs,
Of branches and odds and ends,
Queer little habitations;
And many men lived there all summer.
Sometimes they left this "jungle"
Using the flat-cars mostly,
Many men riding away.
But the autumn was coming; so then
The police of the district decreed
That this place must be destroyed;
Which was done and the hovels burned
And the men distributed
Among hostels in the city
Or in road-building camps in the north
Where they live—in camp or in hostel—
Under regulations;
Disciplined, as if in the army.

II

She left her job in the city,
A well-paying one though it was,
Decided to live in the country
Among the country people.
She thought the city in danger,
Believed that its life was collapsing,
Foundations giving way;
So she rented a cottage near
The outskirts of a village,
Only a few neighbours,
A small and lonely place.
The minds there are those of the country,
Not of the keen city kind,
Though, of course, close to the soil;
And there she does some writing
Along with an effort at gardening.

1933

My Life

(translated from the French of Max Jacob)

The city to be taken is in a room. The booty of the enemy is not heavy and the enemy will not carry it away for he has no need of money since this is a story and only a story. The city has ramparts of painted wood: we shall cut them out and paste them in a book. There are two chapters or parts. Here is a red King with crown of gold who rides on a saw-fish; this is Chapter II: as for Chapter I . . . I no longer remember.

1932

On the Cessation of the Oracles—1

"The well is dry and ceased the babbling water"
From springing into sunlight at the source;
Gone is the trail of that mysterious force,
No priestess telling what the god has taught her.
No smoke ascends from sacrificial altar;
The land deserted has denied its nurse;
There are no ceremonies to rehearse,
And time has put this place to pitiless slaughter.
The attendant nymphs have vanished with the rest.
The god's prophetic mantle is no more.
No Pythia, contorted on the seat,
Strives for an utterance as once before.
The oracle is ceased, no longer blest;
The wreckage of the temple is complete.

1932

On the Cessation of the Oracles—2

At Delphi stand no painted images
Of demi-gods or heroes and the store
Of marble is exhausted from the shore
Of that cerulean sea. The ravages
Of time have long removed the vestiges
Of worship, where the folk no more adore.
The place is nearly as it was before
That shepherd's coming from the villages.
No temples front the high steep rocky ridge
Above the valley for the god is gone
From haunts that once were his and nearby, too,
The muses have fled the friendly sheltered green.
Even the Castalian spring upon the edge
Of that once sacred valley is empty now.

1932

On the Cessation of the Oracles—3

The present extends its arms towards the past
Which holds forth arms reciprocal in vain,
While from the temple close the trees complain
The absence of the nymphs and, all aghast,
The supernatural beings vanish fast;
The deities have fled the smokeless plain,
Fled far away, returning not again,
Faithful although some were until the last.
No white-robed figures from the brighter years
Bewail the fate that long has made them sink.
The desolation of antiquity
Strikes at the heart of things and makes to think
That in the allotting of the happier shares
There is some lack of basic equity.

1932

Martyrs

Saints who were
slaughtered by
wild beasts in
blood-thirsty
Roman
arenas

gasping on
sand that was
red with the
blood of
martyrs

dying looked
upward to
where they had
seen a new
vision of
ecstasy

dying
received a first
glimpse of the
world
celestial.

1929

Punishment

The boys refuse to obey the man. He threatens them, and as they jibe and jeer at him he punishes them.

He whips them in fact by virtue of superior strength. When it is over they jibe and jeer at him again.

He thinks of a stratagem. He will surprise them by kindness. So he begins by letting them have their own way. He smiles at the violence for which he had whipped them, and encourages them to continue it.

The boys do so and jibe and jeer at the man more than ever.

1938

A Little Theosophy Unforseen But Not Unforseeable

(translated from the French of Max Jacob)

The fortifications are paler and more distant. One can no longer make out the gates. It is the time when I think about my dead child. Divorced, remarried, I am a widower and I meditate. O exquisite face of my first wife! She was blonde, she had the candid look of people who have not suffered.

O angelic form of our child; the dead child! Many evenings I have seen again the burial of the child; all the vices went behind the hearse: those that touch the belly, those that touch the forehead, those that touch the thigh, those that touch the foot. There were also one-armed, lame, crippled and blind.

Weep for your dead women! Weep for your beautiful dead child; you would mourn them with less grief if the funeral processions hadn't led to the cemetery the very gargoyles of Notre Dame.

1928

Delphic Apollo

Delphic A-
pollo is
gone from the
haunts that were
sacred in ancient

days in the
morning of
Greece when
light was
supreme.

Can we
discover
here in this
wild clear
rocky region

of the great
foretelling
God some
strong eman-
ation?

1940

Barbizon, France

The Visigoths erected a huge pile
Of massive stones, uncouth and inchoate,
With towers close-set and here and there a gate;
The whole was visible for many a mile.
This was their fortress, this their refuge while
The waves of war were crashing at the gate
And rulers' fates decided. They must wait
Here in a crude but stout-resistant style.
Not far away some shattered ruins lie
Left from an older era ere the day
Of this wild northern flooding on the land;
Among them slender Roman columns stand,
Of well-cut marble, white, toward the sky,—
Warriors no less, but less barbarians they.

1932

To Apollo

Send O
Apollo I
beg, as
once on the
host of

Achaeus
camped on the
plain before
Troy, the
poisonous
arrow

now against
those who would
sweep by
surprise into
that northern
island,

bringing them
into a
not-to-be
mended
disaster.

1926

Hunting Horns

(translated from the French of Guillaume Apollinaire)

Our story's noble, tragical
as is a tyrant's mask.
No chance of drama, magical,
And no indifferent detail
Can make our love pathetical,

And Thomas de Quincy as he drank
The opium poison, gentle, chaste,
To his poor Anne went dreamingly—
Pass on, pass on, since all must pass
I shall often look behind.

Memories are hunting horns
Whose sound is dying on the wind.

1928

The Whippoorwill

When Evening spreads her dusky wings
And shadow covers lake and stream,
What is the bird that, distant, rings?
Only the whippoorwill
Whose lone voice still
Comes forth from woods now dark, once green.

Who calls beneath the rising moon
Over the treetops, past the full,
Companion to the midlake loon?
And who can tell
Its mournful spell
Who has not heard the meaningful

Cry that penetrates the night,
The moon-filled lake, the shores around,
From some lone nook, concealed from sight—
The whippoorwill
Lamenting still
Something lost, and never found.

1940

The Unseen Dwellers

These dwellers in the world of the unseen,—
What are they? Who? Daemons or angels or
The souls of mortals dead? Ever they pour
Into the minds of men a ceaseless stream,
With piercing glances and suggestions keen,—
And are they of the upper or the lower,
These beings surely well-equipped with power
For many things that men have seldom seen.
Let us be wary in our dealings here,—
These beings of the upper rarer air,
Accessible to man in dark seance,—
Room is there much for hope and some for fear—
Are these the wanderers of some region where
Eternal spirits move in glittering dance?

1932

Hope—the Watcher Speaks—1

"Moving through mists of blackness and despair
High, high above the storms of human ill,
That blow relentlessly and bleak and chill,
I saw one star that, radiant, pure and rare,
Beamed in lone splendour through the troubled air,
Like some bright beacon set upon a hill
To guide the weary mariner until
Dawn comes upon the waste of waters bare;
And as I wondered what that star might be,
So clear, so far, yet comforting and kind,
A whisper crept into my waiting mind,
Saying, Behold me, I am Hope, from me
Solace for man's most wretched lot, and cheer."

1932

Incident

The voice claimed to be the mother of the little girl who was asleep upstairs. Her mother was dead recently.

It being dangerous to bring the girl for fear she too should really die, her mother said she would make her dream of her. And after an interval the voice returning said she had done so.

In the morning the little girl was asked had she had any dream in the night, and she answered, Yes, she had dreamed that she was walking in a garden with her mother.

1932

Loon

Black and white
the loon glides at approach of night
on the lake. The moon
nearly full will soon

fill the lake with eerie glow
and the rocks around will soon
echo over the water below
the wild calling of the loon.

1939

Playmate of Old

Playmate of old, seen still in memory,
Where dreary death removed long ere thy prime,
Before thy star its shining course in time
Had well begun;—the changeful lottery
Of life, perchance disdaining to decree
What earthly heights thou wast about to climb,
Thee, with quick turn, to upper realms sublime
Transferred, and merged into eternity.
So must it be as ever it has been;
The young, the beautiful, are early taken;
Thy childish voice, suffused with cheerful light,
Not now for us, alas, on earth forsaken,
Is heard in places where no night is seen
And fills the halls of heaven with delight.

1932

from **We Write Only Our Memories**

(translated from the French of Max Jacob)

At the age of enchantments:—Oh! the palaces in the forests!—I perceived Dante's Beatrice. We were the same age! and my first verses were in praise of her hair without my even daring to have her read them.

At the age of pathos: Oh! the dictionaries, the examinations and the money worries! I saw my Beatrice on the stage of a theatre. Women were sphinxes, I thought: they feed on particular men who are passed to them through the bars of a cage.

At the age of white hair. I—hers was dyed—I met my Beatrice in a drawing room and I spoke to her smilingly of my youth and love:

"Oh! Indeed?" she replied, "that's very curious." And I thought: "The old idiot!"

1945

Moon

How magical
is still water
under the moon
when the moon is full,
her pale image
with some stars too
reflected from
the mirror surface

of silent lake
that bears as well
an island inverted
dark and still,
where the whippoorwill
repeats its call
through the revolving
hours of night;

and all stars circle
the fast-fixed pole,
and the milky way
lies wide across
the sky that enthrones
the queen of night,
the moon above
enchanted water.

1940

Hypocrisy—the Vision

A marble dome I saw, yet small and dim,
Like sainted sepulchres when seen afar,
Under a lowering sky that hid the star
That glows in evening hour at heaven's rim;
Some holy man, methought, with princely whim,
That nothing might his earthly record mar
Had build this dome to last through peace and war
And be on earth a memory of him.
A voice cried out in accents stern and loud;
The dome hath vanished in a cloud of dust;
The voice proclaimed the direful, doleful tale;
Clad in his nakedness and wind-torn shroud
The living dead from out the tomb was thrust;
The sands of time swept on in dreadful gale.

1932

The Creek

The creek, shining,
out of the deep woods
comes with its rippling of
water over pebbly bottom.

Moving between
banks crowded with raspberry
bushes, the ripe red
berries in their short season

to deepen slowly
among tall pines, athletes in
the wind, then the swampy
ground low-lying and damp

where sunlight strikes
glints on the gliding surface
of the clear cold
creek winding towards the shore

of the lake, blue,
not far through reeds and rushes,
where with a plunge, a small
waterfall, it disappears

among the waves
hastening from far to meet
the stranger, the stream issuing
from depths of green unknown.

1944

Over the Water

Over the water
we rowed together,
my father and I,
before the sun
had risen that day—
for we were going
to the narrows
where fish are found.

A chill we felt
the coldness sinking
before the dawn;
it was yet dark;
then, in the twilight,
the islands, the trees,
wan, colourless,
though green by day.

Over the river
we rowed together
oars making ripples
on the smooth surface;
knowing the channels,
passing the islands,
we rowed together
into the dawn.

1927

Canoeing

A steady murmur of water under the bow,
Rippling, rippling;
The canoe glides smoothly along
Straight over the water
Toward the farther shore.
Urge the canoe forward with strong sweeps of the paddle!
The bow leaps;
The ripples multiply;
The water-lily pads glide by more swiftly,
But still silently;
The paddle beats on the gunwhale at the end of each stroke,
Making a drumming sound.
The bow-wave rises higher and higher—
Press hard on the paddle,
Put strength into the stroke!
The canoe is strong. The paddle is strong;
It will not be broken
Though it bend like a bow.
The shore rushes nearer.
Stop paddling now
And let the canoe, losing speed,
Come gently to rest against the muddy bank
In shallow water.

1924

The Image

The image seated across the valley. The path downward and then up. The thick growth on the valley floor. The silence of the deathly valley.

"Let us proceed across the valley making haste for fear of being too late."

The sinking sun is almost down to the crest beyond the valley. The sun sinks inevitably. White clothing will not save the dwellers. They are doomed, must acquiesce.

Up through the stricken air of the early twilight. The sunset persists strangely. The rose of the sky is alive. The image sinks into shadow gradually and those advancing must bring to a stop their restless feet.

1932

Depth

We seek depth.
The surface is not enough.
Depth of experience, feeling.
To dive beneath the surface.
The surface is not enough.
Depth. Into depth.
We make depth, the deep.

1935

The Lake

A beautiful and shining lake there was,
Its surface of a smoothness like a mirror
That had been made and polished without error
Most carefully, of finest moulded glass—
Inviting still the eyes of all who pass
And tempting them to turn and draw yet nearer,
Like siren bold who ravishes each hearer
To lure him on to perish there, alas!
He looked on it who felt temptation's pull
To bathe therein although the banks were high
Snow-covered, cold; this stranger passing by
The peril of the lake was filled with striving,
One moment seen in youthful glory diving,
Then chilled and dead in water beautiful

1932

The Diver

I would like to dive
Down
Into this still pool
Where the rocks at the bottom are safely deep,

Into the green
Of the water seen from within,
A strange light
Streaming past my eyes—

Things hostile;
You cannot stay here, they seem to say;
The rocks, slime-covered, the undulating
Fronds of weeds—

And drift slowly
Among the cooler zones;
Then, upward turning,
Break from the green glimmer

Into the light,
White and ordinary of the day,
And the mild air,
With the breeze and the comfortable shore.

1927

Plunging Into

Plunging into
the shining water
one will feel
a shock of coldness,
sudden, striking
his body's every
part, with the coldness
of northern water.

What does it matter
if northern water
is cold in the summer
and colder in spring,
or if the coldness
of northern water
strikes a chill
that is very chill?

As one plunges
venturesome into,
timorously into
the beautiful water
invitingly lying—
the northern water—
the water is chill,
but what does it matter?

1928

The Treasure

Deep underground there lies a secret store
Of jewels in a cave beside the seas.—
A wanderer would wonder where might be
The path to find that cave along the shore.
When waves in overwhelming volume pour
Into that cave the wariest must flee
Or, by the tide enclosed, cannot get free
But is imprisoned there for many an hour.
His bones will lie beside the water black,
His voice, soon silent, fluttering like a bird
Through the vast spaces of the empty cave
His will shall weaken and his tendons slack
Dissolve. His lower spirit shall be unheard
For he must die and this shall be his grave.

1932

If Birds Are Silent

If birds are silent
at the dawn
something is missing,
something is wrong,
for birds must clamour
before the day,
their song must echo
with the dawn.

The echo of birds'
song with the dawn
must be repeated
each early day;
metallic clamour,
silver-clear,
along with dawn
must strike our ear.

And something is lacking,
something is wrong
if birds are songless
at the dawn.
Where are the birds
that should call in the dawn?
Something is missing
before the day.

1928

The Frog that Wants to Make Itself as Big as an Ox

(translated from the French of Jean de Lafontaine)

A frog looks at an ox
Whose figure seems so beautiful—
Hardly as big as an egg itself—
Envious, it stretches and tries,
Blowing itself up till it's full,
To equal the ox in size,
Saying, "Sister, look at this!
Is this enough? Am I there yet?"
"Naw!" "Now?" "Not at all!" "Here?"
"No, you're not yet anywhere near!"
The wretched creature, by envy accursed,
Blew itself up until it burst.

date unknown

Moeurs Littéraires

(translated from the French of Max Jacob)

The sorcerer's apprentice fidgeted docilely; he smiled with pleasure, looking at his master. He offered himself up to the words of wisdom that were about to gush forth. He didn't resist, he was already swimming in their flow.

The master avowed: "My soul is only a polyp, a sea anemone; I might say it is only a calf's liver in the form of a hand on which an invisible butcher is vainly hacking." "Oh! Master," said the sorcerer's apprentice, "you are plagiarizing Huysmans."

1945

The City

Sweetness of life and sweetness of death. The unbelievable is surely correct. Along the trenches of the understanding runs the electric explosive assault that ends by turning them in a new direction. The others, those that remained, were not capable of the transmutation necessary. In the valley the grass is richer than on the hills surrounding the valley. The assent is difficult and the dangers many and sure. Sure too is the view from the lofty sloping hillside. There is a city in the distance that we had not seen before. There is a city...

1932

The Same—2

Empty of life and sad and desolate
As leafless tree when all the birds are fled,
Or fairy ring when fairies have all sped
Their shrinking footsteps less they be too late,
Or ocean bower of mermaid where one shall wait
In silence the sweet coming of the maid
Who has departed—Where, it is not said—
But may return at some far distant date;—
All kindness, beauty gone, and nothing left
But empty stones to shed salt tears upon—
So is thy dwelling. Now it stands bereft,
Like crown of jewels, or rose-bush of its bloom.
Thy dwelling is as empty as the tomb,
As cold and as forlorn when thou art gone.

1932

To the English Language—1

(after reading some of Dante's sonnets)

Most noble instrument of poetry!
And capable of a true musical note—
Such sounds as flowing from a singing throat
Will come forth marvellous—euphoniously;
Such sweetest sounds, as mingled carefully
Upon the keen translucent air would float
Like silver voices from a silver boat
Joining in ample choir harmoniously.
Thou too art counted among noble tongues
That rule the world, would lead in any duel,—
Though not perhaps Italian or the Greek—
Once sent as scholars to the southern school,
Now capable of utterance pure and clear.
Enchanting tongue! when handled with due care.

1932

The Hammer

The outer shell was quickly broken but the kernel resisted exploitation. This was the true state of things when there arrived on the scene a man with the hammer. He it was who attempted immediately a more drastic assault upon the hidden difficutly. He it was who swung the hammer lustily and eagerly and finally did bring down a resounding whack on the centre of the difficutly. And he it was who saw at once with some dismay that the hammer which he had previously regarded as completely magical had made no impression whatever. This fact caused him and his companions no little trouble in their minds though they tried to pass this off by shouting loudly that the stroke had been completely successful. The wise however were not deceived by this assumption of success and went about making remarks to one another. Meanwhile the core of the difficulty remained as it had been before—completely intact.

1932

The Metals

Loud let the metals clang!
Hammer on iron!
Hammer on steel!
Hammer on brass
Bronze or other metal!
Let them sing in their exultation,
Compelled into shapes that are lasting.
Let them hum and glitter and shriek
And roar in their glee—
The metals!

1924

Summer Day

The alternation of the white and blue
Across the summer day incessantly
Repeats with ever new variety
The ancient pattern that has lasted through
These amiable hours,—with pictures too;—
The lake seen over a valley distantly,
Hills, trees and bushes ordered pleasantly
Make up this prospect that seems ever new.
The clouds have moved a little through the cold
Space above earth and one may gaze around
Until the past is merged into this time.
Fresh memories sown on such earlier ground
Growing together make a newer rhyme,
Make ever old the new and new the old.

1932

Hypno II

"Everybody up there in the north was peeled. Yellow in front. Talk about something, anyway. Please. Seventy-five cents."

"Ran off? Hope? Famed fable." A man was bending somewhat over a couple of listeners and looking to the side.

The idea of a man, or people, devoting self or selves to something. Some watching others, more fortunate. "New opinions don't count." But the idea of something to duplicate the movie stars.

"Have you boon on the Blank mountains?" "Once, only. I saw...." "It was a good thing you weren't swept away in the flood that shook the stars in their courses."

"Be sure and get it strong so that it will last up to the time it is finished. Make a mistake then. Collect-i-hood. It's going to be very bad, unfortunate."

The corresponding heart of England on this occasion. Australia seven years ago.

"Was a man charged high, anything? It was not so good then. Find out where these are wrong."

Even Europe is in flux.

1932

The Watcher Speaks—2

"One night I saw a bright star fall from heaven
Beaming more powerful than many moons,
Like that most fervent sun on hot noons
Bends his strong glance until the hour of even.
Ah! It was fairer than the fabled seven,
The Pleiades, who, with celestial tunes,
Turn in their spheres as smooth as wind-swept dunes
Where keen and polishing winds have strongly striven.
'A spirit is come to earth' I loudly cried,
'Come to make merriment and careless glee,
To drive away the darkness from beside
The hearts of men that sleep and never wake,
To quiet all the winds upon the sea,
And sing the beauty of the mountain lake.'"

1932

The Walk

He walked through the woods
and saw the merging
of the tall trunks
in the green distance—
the undergrowth
of mottled green
with sunlight and shadow,
and flowers starting

here and there
on the mottled ground;
he looked along
the green distance
and up towards
the greenly-laden
curving boughs
of the tall trees;

and down a slope
as he walked onward
down the sloping
ground, he saw
in among
the green, broken,
the blue shimmering
of lake-water.

1928

Island with Trees

The trees are bent
away from the north
on this island
in the lake
wind-swept
in all the seasons—
the northern wind
is master here.

Here the northern
wind is master.
It comes powerful
full and strong
out of the distance
over the water
or over the ice
of the iron winter;

assailing the trees
on the rocky island.
They hold their place
with difficulty,
bent over
by the northern wind,
the savage wind
along the lake.

1928

The Pine

The pine whose noble nature is well-known
I worship now, and take from all the trees
This one to whom I shall bend humble knees,
Unto the pine and unto it alone;
Though there are many other trees, well-grown,
With virtues many, seen in twos or threes;
From some of them my contemplation flees;—
Not from the pine. So let the rest be gone!
This tree stands out from all the woody throng.
See it outlined against the evening sky,
Black against pallid, sharply marked, and know
The pine shall live when all the others die,
Shall be the last survivor of the high
And vigorous forest trees, serene and strong.

1932

There's a Fire in the Forest

There's a fire in the forest!
The creatures are fleeing
The flames close behind
With the wind driving onward.
From underbrush up to
The high moving tree-tops
The fire's surging forward.
There's a fire in the forest;
The whole woods are burning.
The whole world is burning!

The creatures are seeking
The safety of streams
Beyond the hot burning.
The creatures are fleeing;
They are labouring, straining
To reach the cool river
They know just beyond them,
To escape the fierce burning,
To reach the cool stream
For which they are yearning.

date unknown

The Ballad of the Water of the Sea

(translated from the Spanish of Federico Garcia Lorca)

The sea
smiles in the distance.

Teeth of foam.
Lips of sky.

"What do you sell, O troubled young woman,
with breasts to the wind?"

"I sell, señor, the water
of the seas."

"Those saltish tears,
where do they come from, mother?"

"I weep, señor, the water
of the seas."

"Heart, and that grave bitterness,
when is it born?"

"It is most bitter, the water
of the seas!"

The sea
smiles in the distance.

Teeth of foam.
Lips of sky.

1957

Fish

A fish dripping
sparkling drops
of crystal water,
pulled from the lake;
long has it dwelt
in the cool water,
in the cold water
of the lake.

Long has it wandered
to and fro
over the bottom
of the lake
among mysterious
recesses
there in the semi-
light of the water;

now to appear
surprised, aghast,
out of its element
into the day—
out of the cold
and shining lake
the fish dripping
sparkling water.

1928

Du Shönes Fischermädchen

(translated from the German of Heinrich Heine)

You lovely fisher-
Girl.
Bring your skiff to land;
Come to me here
And sit down,
We'll pet here hand in hand.

Lay on my heart your little
Head, without fear
Of me—
Who carelessly trusts yourself
Daily, to the wild sea.

My heart is quite like the sea,
With storm and ebb and flow,
And many a beautiful pearl
Lies in its depth below.

1945

Massacre of the Innocents

(translated from the French of André Salmon)

Children to suicide devoted
Who in the courtyard laugh,
Softest lips and eyelids moist,
White visited by black Love;

A cat's eye serves as candlelight
To gain from books, forbidden,
Seductions chaste and mortal too
So you'll grow big, poor little ones!

Your mothers piously invent
Chastisements quite undefined
For hearts heroic vaguely meant,

Homely children, made handsome by
Promise of nuptial funerals,
Félix, Adolphe, Idoménée!

1945

Hypno II

"You can be sixty, fifty. I was estimating that my interest grew so."

"Jetzt vorwiegend." To little coloured figures on top of a small hill. Light from behind it. Prison walls closing in "and this finance committee slowly. Good, really."

"All that is required is that you don't occupy my room." A lot of people at telephone. Prohibition in U.S.A. "Look, America gambolizes."

"With the idea of failing that first notch." Small wooden house with figure trying to get in.

"They ought to put down some of that wool. Perhaps it was that barrage. The ideal heroine is down on both those practicularies at all."

1932

Vigil—"When to the Sessions"

When in the silent watches of the night
I hear the rain come tapping on the roof,
While kindly sleep holds her soft hands aloof
And Morpheus' ministers have taken flight,—
And all is hidden from the outer sight,
But things within submitted to the proof,
Thoughts and ideas and such inner stuff,
Illuminated by some inner light;—
While at this time the rain taps ceaselessly
My thought flows into memories immured,
In time now past while images rise,
And some that better had remained obscured
Hidden forever from those searching eyes,
Deep-buried in the tomb of memory.

1932

Hypno I

"Pay over your dues before you get caught. We're having you watched, Mr. So-and-So." "And you, are you au fait with these?" A man looks up and says "Yes, sir." It seems odd to Americans that there should be separate terms for all these undoubtedly.

"He's got that far anyway. It was very true, wasn't it?" And I saw the face of a woman. "You won't do anything, will you?"

The doctors were getting ready about her now. A boy was walking away with his mother. A man who might have been his father was in a barber's chair. "Who is going after these men?" "Everybody."

We shall watch for the new magazine." A waiter with white stuff sparkling over his front.

1932

Departure

All is silent now, the rest have gone upon their way.

They were delighted in their time but now a change came over the dream in which they moved and they grew lonely and disinterested.

Return! Only if you return may the master lie again satisfied and dwell in security!

Return! guests who once lived here and brought peace and painted the walls with pictures strange but beautiful.

1938

Hyperion's Song of Fate

(translated from the German of Friedrich Hölderlin)

You stroll above in the light
On softest ground, blessed geni!
Shining divine airs
Touch you gently,
As do the player's fingers
Sacred strings.

Fateless, like the sleeping
Suckling, the heavenly breathe;
Purely preserved
In allotted bud,
The spirit blooms
Ever for them,
And the blessed eyes
Look into still
Eternal clarity.

But to us is given
To rest nowhere,
They vanish, they fall.
Suffering humans,
Blindly from one
Hour to another,
Like water cast year-long
From crag to crag
Down into uncertainty.

date unknown

Picture

The darkening shore
beyond the lake
and over the shore
the glow of the sunset
lingering
but faint and fainter—
the remnant of the
sun that has gone.

Shadows of darkness
fall on the water;
an island looming
across the glow
with evergreens
against the sunset,
tall, continuous,
and dark.

The sunset glowing
far in the west
but faint and fainter
seems to expire;
over the dark
thin band of shore
the dim remembrance
of the sun.

1930

One Leaf

One leaf is
floating on
ripples in
shallow
shore-side
water

over the
sand at the
bottom that
shimmers in
sunlight

where the leaf's
shadow lies
motionless
almost
there on the
flat sand

among the
swift-moving
bright
refractions of
sunlight.

1929

The Bell

A bell was ringing. Through the air came the sound of other bells while the moonlight spread over the stone steps. The queer man with the black hat watched the moon. Stars sparkled with intensity. If an angel was singing somewhere no one heard it. After an hour there was silence because the bells had stopped ringing. Down the stone steps came a number of people. After a time the moon was down and still the stars sparkled.

1928

Trees and Moon

The trees seem richer tonight.
Perhaps it is because of the full of the moon.
The moon behind the trees.
The full moon behind the beeches and the elms.
The maples and the full moon.
The moon's round is cut by the blackness of branches.
The sharpness of leaves—black.
Abode of what, of whom?
Moon, abode of whom?

date unknown

By the River

This water runs so smoothly and the green
Reflected in it so distinctly shows
It must appear to one at hand he knows
That he, below, another world has seen
There in the water's heart, where in between
The upper and the low the surface glows
Without a flaw. Above, the summer glows
As we together watch the stream serene.
The day is delightful on this river shore
And in the sunlight everything is near.
The river in silence at our feet has made
Its course, it seems, forever and an hour,
While death, in the distance, meaningly may nod
And whisper to us. But we shall not hear.

1932

Pine Gum

The white gum showing
in the gloom
among the massive
trunk of a great
pine tree standing
on the hill,
with a deep bed
of needles below;—

scarcely a breeze
along the hill;
scarcely a current
of morning air
to make the pine's
old melody,
for it is evening;
the air has ceased

its daily stirring;
the light grows dimmer
within the shadow
of the pine,
but ever appears
through the darkness
the ghostly glimmering
of the gum.

1929

Young Poplars

The breeze rustles
the poplar leaves,
whitish-surfaced,
conspicuous;
they seem to twitter
and chatter always;
the young trees
are never still.

1930

When One Comes

When one comes to the end one stops.
There is no going farther.
The garden sights are mingled with odours.
The garden colours, intense.
Daffodils and crocuses appear first, and narcissi—
You have lily of the valley.
Perhaps here are poppies, an edge of poppies.
The end of the garden is a wall.
One must stop at the end.
To watch and pray in the garden.

1930

The Fact

The sweetness of the mere fact cannot be held within the mind, but must be sent outward and so communication and sympathy will be established. But there are some who may deny all reality, even the plainest, preferring to keep themselves within the rigid contours of outmoded seats of thought, where thought dwelt once but no longer; where the acute eye can perceive now only remnants, dust, and a dullness too. Some indeed prefer to remain within that zone—but the events cannot wait on loiterers.

1932

Mystery Initiation

There is a narrow passageway.
One can touch the walls on either side.
There are difficulties, obstacles;
yet one must advance.
There is water to cross, wading deeply and more deeply.
It must be terrifying.
It is sure to be terrifying
there in the darkness.
If anything is seen, it is unpleasant, even terrifying.
There are angry visions.
There is fire.
There is fire.
Yet one must advance.
The passage is narrow, tortuous.
One is frightened, one must not be frightened.
The light of the sun is far off.
Yet one may arrive at light.
Through darkness into light.
One must pass through terror into light.

1930

Apparition

Why did a grass-snake lustrous green
So sinuously glide
Out from the sumacs' sheltering screen
To come and pause beside
The pine tree by whose roots I sat
Astonished suddenly by that

Apparition from beyond
My word of everyday?
Its nimble tongue shot forth unbound
In rapid threatening play.
Its slim length twisted silently
As on the ground it softly lay—

When, doubling quickly, it returned
Upon its former track
As if a hostile glance had spurned
An innocent attack,
Refused whatever gift it brought—
Or what strange purpose was its thought.

1940

Moonlight

The moonlight on the river.
The moon comes every month.
The yellow light. Is it yellow?
The reflection of the moon in the water.
It is broken by the ripples.
The stillness.
Is the river moving?
Is the river asleep?
Is the world, too, asleep?

1932

The Curtain

Peering into the dim curtain we can make out certain figures which move towards us and then away as though vacillating between a desire for contact with us and the contrary. Finally however as they emerge, becoming clearer, it is perceived that we have known them too, and that there in the next stream, the next street, are swimmers, or walkers, not so very unlike ourselves.

1932

Recognition

If you are she whom I have never known
Except in dreams under a different light
From that of day, far in the secret night,
When outward I is silent and alone;
At those still times of dreaming when are gone
Day's sudden fits, and souls are free for flight
Even to the edge of rare and new delight—
Though the edge only till they are full grown—
If you see within dream's chambered towers
Looking to spaces where no darkness is,
By what sign shall I know you in the hours
Of dull dark day, upon the common street?
And what shall tell me secretly that this
Is she whom I only in dreams did meet?

1932

Cicadas

Shrill from the
pines comes the
sound of the
tree-loving
singing cicadas

answering
as if an
echo
arose now
here and now
yonder.

From tree to
tree they
respond in this
warm and
sunlit
noonday—

spirits of
heat, with their
keen dry
unseen
singing.

1940

Love's Silver Bells

Love's silver bells shall ring to call
The sleeper from his sleep,
And he shall speedily know all
The mystery of that deep

Wherein his spirit shall begin
A journey strange and dim
Where everything will straightway seem
Enchantment dear to him.

For, bound within a hollow cell
In older custom's chain,
He did not hear the silver bell—
His deafness was in vain!

The sound struck softly on his ear;
What can he do—oh, then—
But rise alert, at once, to hear
This music known to men

Of old, the music that was heard
Beyond antiquity,
And sweeter than the call of bird
In spring's ubiquity.

1932

The Spring

We hear the spring from far across the lake
There, invisible, for when silence holds
All—and the evening too—
The ear extends its view

Deep into regions not attained by day
Now opening to the searching heedful ear
Which presently has found
That source of spreading sound.

The ear is awakened to subtlest inner tones
And the wideness of the world is opened too.
It knows a flow begun
Under an earlier sun,

And it is attuned to beauty in delicate sound
As seldom in the noisier light of the day,
Aware now of the spring
As a more audible thing.

Stepping into a boat we may set out
To find the spring, following by the murmur
In darkness growing more
Towards the farther shore.

As we draw near, over the evening lake,
In the hush the sound is more audible than before
But unintelligible,
Not understood well

As of some creature held in a spell and striving
To be free of that bondage, impotent however,
And uttering a complaint
Although its means are faint;

As if attempting to speak and not succeeding
But strangled in utterance, making that utterance vain;
Yet only brief must be
This disability

Of words enchanted to meaninglessness, yet once
Filled with meaning, and perhaps once again
These syllables of fire
To meaning may aspire,

Be understood. Ours is the lack of hearing.
Our ear will hear again and there will be joy
Among the dwellers round
This source of secret sound,

That once again, after long interval—
Ours is the error; we cannot comprehend—
We again may understand
The springs beneath the land.

1933

Visitation

(translated from the French of Max Jacob)

My room is at the back of a courtyard and behind shops. No. 7 Ravignan Street, you remain the chapel of my eternal memory! I have lain there thinking, stretched out on the couch supported by four bricks; and the owner has pierced the zinc roof to increase the light. Who knocks so early in the morning?—Open! Open the door! Don't get dressed!—Lord!—The cross is heavy; I want to put it down.—How can it come in? The doorway is so narrow!—It will come in through the window.—My Lord! Warm yourself! It is so cold.—Look at the cross!—Oh Lord! All my life.

1932

The Nimble Fish

So suddenly the nimble fish will strike
After long stalking on the bottom low
Within the stream whose waters swiftly flow
That his attack upon the bait is like
The pouncing of the bitter northern shrike
On little bird who yields beneath the blow
Whose keen eyes dimming lose their former glow—
The surface breaks; it is a full-grown pike,
Who has taken the bait, and now repents perhaps
Too late, too late! Live fish, the time is past
For you to plunge and play among the reeds.
Now you must come forth gasping with fevered flaps
Of gills, and struggle till the very last
Is done, for when fate speaks each strong fish heeds.

1932

The Open Door

The open door closing and the closed door opening made the entrance only so much easier for the way lay between the past and the present, seemingly. So the two new guardians of the twin towers seeing draw near the enemy may make off in spite of all their pretensions to a superior kind of bravery. They are indeed cowardly ever—these guardians of the closing and opening door, but there they are and who shall remove them? Let the passage be difficult, that makes no difference, to them or us. The door clangs shut perhaps and then below the tower we hear the sound of horsemen galloping along the road. Far off along the road we know the other horsemen are coming, but will they arrive before the door is closed? Can these depart before the door is opened?

1932

The Shadow

This shadow could not be more dense,
more opaque.
Light would have difficulty penetrating it.
It is like a fog.
It is solid as a fog.
Fogs are sometimes blown away.
They are dissipated
They are dissolved by the sunlight attacking from above.
Even darkness may be dissipated.

1932

Blindness

If I am blind, do not encumber me
With any talk of beauty's trappings dull
Or anything superfluous else, or full
Of wind and vain—such things are not for me;—
Or any tales of islands in the sea
Or lands of much entrancement, beautiful,
Or music, colours no less wonderful
That are where beauty's residence may be;
But let me move most scornfully among
The relics of a long since ancient land;
Why incommode oneself to such extent
As to see wonders in a simple song
Or to be wrapped in musings sweet or stand
Amazed before an empty monument.

1932

Rocky Bay

The iron rocks
slope sharply down
into the gleaming
of northern water,
and there is a shining
to northern water
reflecting the sky
on a keen cool morning.

A little bay—
and there the water
reflects the trees
upside down,
and the coloured rock,
inverted also
in the little
shining bay.

Above, on the rock,
stand trees, hardy,
gripping the rock
tenaciously.
The water repeats them
upside down,
repeats the coloured
rock inverted.

1930

Intrusion

No musical or other sound may intrude within these walls and silence here is king. The one retreat from all that makes for din, for shattering of glass and breaking of many bubbles. Enter, but not with too great haste. Regret, regret will come and may return like old year's pain. Regret, even, will enter here on stealthy feet and so disturb the lasting calm.

1932

Reality

In its green solidity
Very real is every tree;
Very clear is the outline
Of each one of the leaves that shine

In the sunlight. A cylinder
Is every trunk, and circular,
Nearly, does each leaf gleam.—
Earth, then, is not a dream.

The objects in the countryside
Are solid heavy and opaque.
The road runs resolutely on.
These exist. Let no mistake

Confuse the mind but there are here
Objects real and very clear;—
And yet this tree is designed free
From empire of geometry.

1928

The Saws Were Shrieking

The saws were shrieking
and cutting into
the clean white wood
of the spruce logs
or the tinted hemlock
that smells as sweet—
or stronger pine,
the white and the red.

A whirling saw
received the logs;
the sound was ominous
and shrill,
rising above
the sullen roaring
of the mill's machinery

From the revolving
of the saw
came slices of clear wood
neatly sawn,
white pine and red,
or spruce and hemlock,
the sweet spruce,
and the sweet hemlock.

1929

The Old Chinaman

The old Chinaman
in the laundry
near the corner
always smiles
as I bring in my shirts.

The Chinese, it seems
are always smiling.
Perhaps they're trained
to keep on smiling
as if to prove
they're not afraid
of tigers in doorways
around the corner.

Years and years
the old Chinaman
smiling, smiling.
I've grown older
quite a lot
but he hasn't got any
older at all.

1958

Explanation

It is very simple. You take a step forward and face a mirror. Then the reflection from behind meeting that mirror on its way back is transferred forward towards the next mirror in the series. In the meantime you perceive another mirror beyond the first and the process is repeated. Or it is like a series of chambers. As you pass from one to the next, you realize that the second one contained the first. And so on. There are other ways too of representation besides the progression of mirrors or the progression from one chamber to the next. Among them is the.....

1932

The Subtle Odour

The subtle odour exhaled by certain blossoms being able, as is known, to attract insects the woods were vibrant although as is also known the light spring flowers possess very little odour. Yet the air expectant received the attention of cloud shadows. A walker came to the edge of the woods and looked around. An early meadowlark was out in the field. Night! Night! The spring sunlight and after it some rain. The walker knew the circumstances of this season and sniffed the air. Some of the trees were more powerful than others. The rays of the sun however found no difficulty in passing their opposition.

1931

Blue Flowers

Blue flowers
by the road
growing in
stateliness
many together

All erect
in the air
thrusting their
blue-bearing
stems—

And so we
stopped to pick
some of these
blooms by the
roadside.

Breaking off
several
then, we
collected a
handful.

1926

We Saw No Sign

We saw no sign of death
there on the edge of death.
Death awaiting
gave no mark, no indication,
of his sudden coming.
Death creeps from behind,
and is abruptly
in full sight like an apparition
scarcely realized
until it has vanished
leaving
the fact the silence,
only the silent fact.

1935

Sounds

Magical
ever the
sounds on the
wild hill
here by the
water,

shrill high
tones of the
tree-dwelling
unseen ci-
cadas,

calls of birds,
rustling of
leaves on the
oak or the
beech or the
basswood—

nearer than
all, the
constant low
sound of the
pines.

1940

Not in the Stream

Not in the stream
rapidly flowing can we drown
but beyond, in the lake
stagnant, ominous,
with the bottom of mud
and the quietness
ever.

After the rush
and the swift descent
over the stony bed
and the narrow places
the dull quiet
of the reedy lake.

1935

Islands of Song

Islands of song, where the shrill veering winds
Are never known, and never the keen frost
Has come relentlessly with shivering host
Of ghostly snowflakes, and where no man finds
Other than speech melodious from minds
Attuned to beauty that was never lost
Or by the streams of dull stupidity crossed
But yet is living as the light that blinds—
Would I were there! And yet where are those isles,
Where are those archipelagoes of song?
And who can find them, or do they appear
But in the fancy's dim and furtive smile?
Sunken into forgetfulness for long
Where are those islands that have been so near?

1932

The Last Visit

(translated from the French of Max Jacob)

The old maid!

She wears a black silk cape; she arrives with her lameness which supports her words and her hollow laugh.

She comes into the garden, descending its scarcely marked slope.

They thought she was lying down, very ill.

"Well, since the doctor doesn't come to me, I'm coming to you, and I wish to say that I died this morning at . . . but I can't find the words any more . . . Excuse me . . . if you see a flame in a bowl, it isn't melted candle wax, it's my soul . . . yes, indeed!" laughing, always amiable.

"Good health to you all! I'm going away."

1932

Death of the Devil

The devil was dead. There was no doubt about it. Enlightenment said so, the latest philosophy said so. Scientists proved it. It was laughable, the idea the devil might still be alive at all, to say nothing of being strong enough to exhibit some inclination to maleficient activity, such as torturing, flaying, burning, shooting, promiscuous murder, destruction of cities by fire and chemicals, propagation of lies, slavery for men and the horrible laughter of the heartless and the powerful, etc., etc.......

Since the devil was so very dead they held the funeral. It lasted over a good many years with much laughter and sneerings at the back-water individuals who stupidly refused to see that he was indeed dead and that progress was to rule forever more. Such old fogies almost deserved to be buried with him they in a sense so much resembled. Much was written about the demise of the devil, in the form of pamphlets, books, articles, etc., etc., proving that since man had left the monkey far behind the same laws that had made man what he is also ensured that what was best would come to the front willy-nilly, for whatever is the strongest is the best.

However, just when the obsequies seemed to have been concluded a false and discordant noise arose, like the whisper of a rather sinister mechanical monster a long way off behind a hill. It was the hill of hell, in fact. Before anyone realized what had happened or could raise even a finger and thumb to snap them, all the murdering, flaying, torturing was rampant again, more violent, stronger than ever. The devil was out again, unmistakably, and he brought with him all the etc., etc..........

To the considerable surprise of onlookers and prophets of progress whose fantasies took a new and surprising tune, in fact were abruptly jerked out of existence.

1944

Sun

Hail to thee
sun of the
world in the
morning
calmly rising

Hail to thee
great sun
nobly
accoutred in
splendour

We that are
mortals
acclaim thee
master of
light and of
living.

Hail thee from
darkness
here, from the
dark small
earth.

1918

Autumn Maples

Beautiful
colours though
not the most
varied
hues of the
rainbow

Autumnal,
repeating this
season a
part of the
spectrum

All of the
woods are flam-
boyant with
fabulous
hues of the
maple

Surely this
gay display
cannot be
hinting of
death?

1958

Moon-House

Out of the painted porticoes
        there is a streaming
The house of the moon
        There is an old castle
But why turn turn continually?
They burn, they burn—
And the moon
        The borrowed lighting
Has gone and the moon—
        Let me see perpetual
delightings and sustained rejoicings.

1932

Passage

He passed through death
and when he came
to the other side
he was the same,
he was the same
as he was before
he passed through
death's door

1923-29

Death

<table>
<tr><td></td><td>is it</td></tr>
<tr><td>dark</td><td></td></tr>
<tr><td>is it</td><td>black</td></tr>
<tr><td></td><td>is it</td></tr>
<tr><td>black</td><td>is it</td></tr>
<tr><td></td><td>dark</td></tr>
<tr><td>is it</td><td>dark?</td></tr>
</table>

1927

July 20 1944

"Half-past war and all's hell!" called out the watchman on his rounds among the ruined city where the uninterred corpses rose trembling to their feet to shake hands which glowed with an eerie phosphorescence among the broken arches of cathedrals. A twenty-tonne jet-propelled flying bomb descending from the stratosphere into a cemetery scattered skulls to a distance, maximum, of one hundred and sixty-five miles. One lit through an open window of a three-hundred-year-old palace into a plate of soup being enjoyed by a general whose moustache was splashed unceremoniously.

Twenty corpse-laden submarines, colliding under water, simultaneously astonished the well-known denizens of the deep who, however, after scattering in terror, returned at length to consume a well-merited meal.

Two tanks climbed the twin towers of Schlopfenhegel Cathedral, one to each, without slowing down, and rose from the tops simultaneously in a perfectly hypberbolical trajectory to bury themselves one hundred feet deep in the back garden of Professor Slypuss the well-known mechanical wizard who was at the moment seated before the fire making a calculation leading to an amplified weapon of defence which would destroy at one time a city of one hundred and three thousand instead of doing it in the usual four sections or instalments.

Three famous Darwinians were annihilated by an oildrum filled with hydrocyanic acid while in the midst of a compilation designed to show how successfully humanity was adapting itself to rapidly and not too agreeably changing external circumstances.

A special excursion from the capital city of hell brought twenty thousand curious devils up to view a spectacle which exceeded their hardiest anticipations. His satanic majesty acknowledged himself "most favourably impressed by the state of affairs which in some ways went beyond his fondest hopes."

The general merriment was added to by the sight of a strayed angel hastily trying to escape upward with wings badly singed by an exploding anti-aircraft shell.

1944

Canto 101

(E.P. in Heaven)

Here I am, lodged in "eternal bliss."
The place is well enough built
but draughty.
A certain sameness
About it all. Looking
In every direction only
The same sort of people,
and all highly respectable.
And we have seen all that there is to be seen
And we are a little bored.
These endless praises.
Why should one sing and sing?
And I spoke to one lady about this
And she said: "You're telling me!"
(And she an angel, too.)
And I have had enough of these endless singsongs,
This perpetual chorale, voices out of tune,
Haloes askew, and sloppy wings.
When I look at them
I think there's no one duller
Than the typical angel.
The song runs on
but I am tired of it.
And the architecture? Much too old fashioned.
Chrysoprase? Bah! Emerald? Bah!
And they were building another "pearly gate,"
And I sez to St. Peter:
"Who's the *ciptain?* on this job?"

An' *he* sez: "You can't fool me!
I'm onto all them *dago* words,
So don't go on callin' no names around here!"
And Chin Wang spoke from the ether,
"The sunset comes every day.
                    So does the dawn.
And if you can't wobble that pivot
                                        then don't!"
And I stood on the parapet
                              admiring his profundity.
Meant! Meant! Papiols! The old days
                                        in the South!
A castle of stone
                    not bejewelled
                    and not dull
Io! Io! Aoi!
A brief light
                    but golden
A moving brightness
                    held in the ether-air.

And how can one write
Without pen or paper
Or even a typewriter?

And there is no variety in this place.

1953

Two Poems

(And not by E. P.)

An' Adam sez:
"Whatizat?"
An" Eve sez: "Don't you know?
'At's a apple."
AND
Adam and Eve looked at the apple
And the apple was there
And they looked, and Adam looked
And Eve looked
at the apple
And the apple got bigger and bigger
And the apple got smaller and smaller
And the apple was still there
On the tree
And YOU try
to make anything
out of
this

1955

(Also not by W.C.W.)

This red apple
Let me
Look
at
it

I'm looking
Now

So what? It's just
an apple
after
all

1955

The Boat Ride

Come ride in a boat past the shelving shore where the castle stands ruined and the ruins of the castle show sharp and black in the moonlight. Let us glide beyond the ruins, beyond the headland on which the castle once stood, around the headland past the sleeping village with the roofs of the houses shining a little in the moonlight; and going on as the boat glides down with the stream, on its dark surface, we may come at length to the land that we left once; and we may come to that land about dawn.

1944

Editor's Endnotes

Eustace Ross wrote by hand, working in notebooks. His habit was to work for a while on a translation, and then as his urges and intuitions flagged, to take up another notebook — new imagist poems — and work on those, and then, I suppose if he was having a really good day, to switch books and tone-up a sonnet or two. I've known only one other writer who worked like this — who also wrote by hand in notebooks — and that was James T. Farrell, who would work on four or five novels at once. To reflect Ross's habit of mind — and to deflect the idea that he was strictly an imagist with an eye only for pine gum and cold water — I have not ordered the poems chronologically (as did the editors of *Shapes and Sounds*, 1966, given what they had in hand), but I have placed sonnets beside the surreal, translations from the French beside the German and Latin and Spanish, and all in the context of his on-going imagist verse. There are periods in which he seems to have written every day (culminating in a great burst in 1932), periods of fits and starts, and periods of length when he wrote nothing at all.

His notebooks and loose papers are a hodge-podge, and there are hundreds of still undeciphered handwritten poems, partial poems, almost complete translations in his pinched, hard to read script. They are in some 44 boxes in the Robarts Library. It is my belief that not only Ross's work needs to be looked at with a fresh eye, but through him, the beginnings of modern verse in Canada.

In 1955, Ross, in response to a piece written by William Carlos Williams, sat down in his attic and wrote a letter. It was a hurried letter. He wrote about poetry in the way he would talk about poetry to another poet. Some sentences are awkward and repetitive, and sometimes he sounds like a plumber talking about elbow joins and fittings. He decided not to send it. He tried to shorten it, and then to use it as the basis of an article. Then he abandoned it. Still, given the seemingly easy directness of so much of his verse, it is interesting to see how hard he worked over complicated matters of stress and meter in his head.

62 Delaware Avenue,
Toronto, Ontario, Canada
May 11, 1955

Dear Dr. Williams,

Your statement and letter to Cid Corman in Origin X!! aroused my keen interest and I have finally decided that I really must send you some comments,—though a stranger to you, personally. Not to your writing, though, poetry or prose either. Morley and Loretto Callaghan, friends of ours for many years, have often spoken of you. Once when we (my wife and I) were driving, or rather being driven, back from New York we went thirty miles or so out of our way to go through Paterson, N.J. because of my interest in a poem of yours, "Paterson," in The Dial. This trip was in the early thirties. Miss (Marianne) Moore, with whom I have corresponded on and off since The Dial days — and met once on one of our very few visits to New York — informed us that she had told you of this incident!

Now, when you say, "I among the rest have much to answer for," (speaking of lack of 'measure'), I have only to open a book in front of me now, your Collected Poems, 1921-1931, The Objectivist Press, to disagree. Poem after poem shows what I would certainly call 'measure'. In those two-three-or four-lined stanzas the lines may not 'scan' regularly, it is true, but there is 'balance' in the varying lengths of the lines, — and I think balance implies measure? And aren't the stresses in a line fundamental?

To be specific, let me examine "The Source". (May I say that for some reason or other 'water in an old hoof print' occurs to me frequently, especially in the country?) In the first stanza there are three lines and three stresses in each. In the second there are three stresses in the first line, two in the second, and this is very appropriate, just right. Right, too, is the longer next line to which I give five stresses (usually) rather than four. And so on. The number of stresses in a line is surely a 'measure'. Its variation from line to line, if done rightly, gives a 'balance' effect. If you wish, you can say that a line with three stresses has three 'feet', etc., but the variety of feet that would eventually have to be defined might exceed in number those devised by the later classical grammarians in analyzing the choruses of Euripides, etc! So I use the word 'stress' (or sometimes 'beat') rather than 'foot', in talking of less standard forms, at least.

You say, again, "We have today to do with the poetic, as always, but a relatively stable foot not a rigid one." And, later, "Such a foot . . . may consist of one syllable . . . or even a dozen." Doesn't the idea of 'stress' come close to that of 'a variable foot'? I don't know the maximum number of syllables a stress can carry but for an example of the minimum, turning again to "The Source," 6th line, 'few' and 'light' can each be taken as one foot if stress be placed, as is natural, on each.

When you say, "Most poems I see today are concerned with what they are saying, how profound they have been given to be," I would concur. Certainly a current tendency, very marked indeed in at least one 'little magazine', is to give attention only to the meanings of the words, with the object of cramming a maximum number of connotations — imagery, metaphor, even a sort of punning at times — into a set of words. This aspect is important, of course, but tends to be overdone if theoretically exaggerated. (Cf, Abraham Cowley's 'wit-poetry.') In poetry long preserved, 'measure', 'balance', the metrical structure, the actual sound of the words, has obviously played a most important role. As for metaphor, there is the method, which I myself favour, of making the whole poem — if a short one — rather than only details, a sort of metaphor.

Again, widely, disjointedness (in form) has become a convention and the form is not compelled by the content, does not fuse with it. Poetry might be defined as writing that shows form compulsion. The poetry comes when matter and form are fused. Even the images, metaphors etc., must fit into the matter-form fusion somehow. Many ignore this requirement. We now have either what looks like a piece of the Cantos attacked by an axe, or else something that resembles blank verse but isn't; the 'sprawl' of a series of lines whose scanning is ambiguous. (5 feet or 4? One seldom knows.) 'Unbalanced' (or 'unmeasured') 'free verse' (I'll still use that term, here), approaches prose, not good but bad prose.

Stress-balance can 'carry' short stanzas (I say 'can' because obviously that is the case with many of your pieces) and a not too long series of short stanzas. There remains the question of longer stanzas and also of length in general. Continuous irregular unrhymed verse (blank verse is unrhymed of course but regular), depending on stress-balance presents such difficulties as practically to omit it in length. Wallace Stevens' short pieces are of interest from the point of view of stress-balance. With length, he tends toward blank verse. "The Man with the Blue Guitar" is a notable exception, and there is one rhyme that repeats itself in the two-line four-footed, or stresses, stanzas' series, 'guitar' and 'are'.

Regarding stanzas for longer poems there is a very interesting method as you know, namely, definitions of the number of syllables in each line of the stanza. This method was, I think, first used extensively by Marianne Moore, though there may be at least one piece by Pound of this type, and Dylan Thomas adopted it with success, as in "Vision and Prayer," and "Poem in October." Here we have 'measure' undoubtedly. (The number of stresses in corresponding lines, however, may and does vary though the number of syllables may be the same.) If the language ever goes 'dead', future scholars will have no difficulty in understanding the metrical principle of this verse, even though without knowledge of the stresses they may not know how it sounded. (Compare the situation with Greek, the accents, etc.) Of course, tape-recording may preserve the sound of verse, with the stresses, etc., indefinitely? Cid Corman seems enthusiastic now about it. (See Origin XV)

It seemed to me some time ago, and for a long period, that verse of definite structure, measure, though unrhymed

— resembling 'free verse' superficially — would be 'North American' in feeling, or could be. This 'North American' feeling was, as I remember, provoked or stimulated in particular by a piece by Marianne Moore in The Dial, late in 1924, I think, starting "an octopus/ of ice". If I may be permitted to speak of my own efforts, let me say that, regarding experimentation, this consciously, in my own case, in 1925, when I found myself discontened with 'free verse' which I could do little with, I set about investigating definite unrhymed patterns. My pieces have appeared in Canadian anthologies, to some extent, but only rarely, once or twice in The Dial and Poetry (Chicago), in the United States, so I may be pardoned for this attempt to send one or two of my ideas, for what they are worth, across the border. I have been very lax about trying to secure publication in book form, and now think I made a mistake.

After some trials based on a study of Greek and Latin stanza forms I resorted to the 'laconics' or '2-beat' form, in 1925. A number of these 'laconics' were (privately) printed in a small book in 1930. In them the guiding idea was a 'ground-rhythm' maintained by having two stresses or 'beats' in each line of the stanza, and 8 as the number of lines increased, which gave, for me, a distinct 'balance' or 'cadence' that seemed essential. With a ground rhythm established, 'forced stress' can come into play. Can the ear 'be jogged out of its boredom' by a variation in the relationship between the number of syllables and the (established) number of stresses? This was, in a way, the theory on which the 'laconics' were based. These 'laconics' seemed to me to be 'North American'. However, I found this stanza (form) applicable effectively only to quite short pieces.

I'm sorry the examples (enclosed) happen to be mostly 'nature', which by no means limits the themes of pieces I have written. Examples of 'forced stress' might be pointed out. Since there are two beats in each line, and these come to be expected, stress, may be thrown on the word <u>desire</u>. (For example, in "The Saws Were Shrieking", second last line, 'sweet' is stressed, by the metrical 'habit', so to speak. 'And shrill' too. In "Falling Water", note 'far springs'. Both words must be stressed. In "Cedar Leaf," 'of the wild' — extra stress or emphasis is thrown on 'wild' because it can't very well fall on 'of the'. In "The Walk", (instead of, 'the blue shimmering', 'The blue shining' wouldn't do. Shimmering has extra syllables and these are I think necessary in giving the effect wanted. In "The Fish", 'cool' and 'cold' must both be stressed. 'Recesses' carries the weight of a whole line and gains effect thereby. 'Into the day' — 'day' carries extra stress, and so is made more effective.)

In the 'allegro' pieces, which I used to call 'light sixes', we have simply hexameters and pentameters, under the influence of the ancients (Greeks) plus e.e. cummings (early in 1926).

This effort at producing short forms ended practically speaking in 1930, when I wrote a couple of longer pieces in the last form illustrated, which I call '3's, which seems capable of some continuity or length. (This is used by Robert Frost in the "Sound of Wind".) Since then I have — apart from rhymed verse and blank verse, or near blank — used almost exclusively the patterns of 1925-30, or modified. The first 1925 (the more classical, no examples) have proved most useful in translation from the Romans or Greeks.

As for forms suitable for longer pieces of verse, I have thought about that a good deal, but results are rather indefinite. (In long pieces made up of stanzas there must be some sort of continuity, each stanza should, somehow, lead naturally to the next.) Speaking generally, I have found a slight injection of rhyme rather necessary.

I think 'balanced' free verse is at its best in Hölderlin. He often used a particular four-line stanza pattern, evidently based on classical models. "The Arctic" is in this form.

The search for poetic forms may be compared to mining. The veins are there, somehow. They are the forms. Innovators, prospectors, find and sometimes develop, exploit them. The great poets are liable to exhaust the veins they work on. But sometimes the same form, after centuries perhaps, may come back into effective employment. The vein is rich again farther on. An example is the Spenserian stanza which seemed worked out, 'dead', but was used successfully by Byron with a different 'slant' to it (and rather, as I think, unsuccessfully by Shelley). There is always the chance of coming on new veins.

I confess myself long-winded on this subject at least, and had better close before you are too bored to continue reading!